NO MORE LIVES CUT SHORT

The Australian Women's Health Diary
funds breast cancer clinical trials research
to save and improve the lives of
every person affected by breast cancer.

Today, tomorrow and forever.

Giving back futures

Every day this year, it's expected that 57 people will hear the words "you have breast cancer". The shock, anguish and fear this will inflict on the lives of so many is hard to imagine. I'm sorry if you've ever heard those words.

Lives will be changed forever and sadly, despite our advances, lives will be lost and family and friends left heartbroken. Enough is enough.

What do we need to do to stop deaths from breast cancer? When I ask the researchers at Breast Cancer Trials, they tell me we need more clinical trials research.

We need to take laboratory advances to clinical trials at the earliest opportunity, to identify personalised treatment for every person, and to break down the funding barrier, which is holding back the research that could save people's lives and give them back their futures.

Your purchase of this diary is helping. Thank you for giving hope to those who have lost their loved ones, to people who are going through breast cancer now or who live with the physical and emotional scars of their experience, and to all the families who bravely support them.

We stand together with the women who feature in this diary – who have been through so much and yet are hopeful that, with more clinical trials research, the future will be different for their children and for other women, too.

My wish is that you benefit from the wonderful health information this diary has to offer, and that your 2025 is fabulous!

Lisa x

LISA WILKINSON

**BREAST
CANCER
TRIALS**

*Imagine a world without breast cancer…
Now imagine that in your lifetime*

A breast cancer diagnosis is devastating. It doesn't matter how
old you are; no one expects to have their life put at risk.

Everyone wants and deserves their future.

In Australia, nine women still lose their life to breast cancer every day,
leaving heartbroken families and friends behind.

Every one of them matters.

It is the most commonly diagnosed cancer in the world – every minute
of every day, another person is being told they have breast cancer.

Breast cancer is cruel. It is complicated and we don't have all the answers.

We need more solutions for every person, every situation, every time.

Clinical trials research is the proven pathway to get
new breast cancer treatments to patients and those at risk.

We have a bold ambition for a future where no one dies from breast cancer.

Where no more lives are cut short.

It's going to take time, passion, new ways of thinking, inspiration, determination and
a community behind us, but we won't give up until no more lives are cut short.

Thank you for buying this diary.

THE TEAM AT BREAST CANCER TRIALS

FIND OUR MORE AT BREASTCANCERTRIALS.ORG.AU OR SCAN THIS CODE

Calendar
2025

JANUARY

S	M	T	W	T	F	S
			1	2	3	4
5	6	7	8	9	10	11
12	13	14	15	16	17	18
19	20	21	22	23	24	25
26	27	28	29	30	31	

FEBRUARY

S	M	T	W	T	F	S
						1
2	3	4	5	6	7	8
9	10	11	12	13	14	15
16	17	18	19	20	21	22
23	24	25	26	27	28	

MARCH

S	M	T	W	T	F	S
30	31					1
2	3	4	5	6	7	8
9	10	11	12	13	14	15
16	17	18	19	20	21	22
23	24	25	26	27	28	29

APRIL

S	M	T	W	T	F	S
		1	2	3	4	5
6	7	8	9	10	11	12
13	14	15	16	17	18	19
20	21	22	23	24	25	26
27	28	29	30			

MAY

S	M	T	W	T	F	S
				1	2	3
4	5	6	7	8	9	10
11	12	13	14	15	16	17
18	19	20	21	22	23	24
25	26	27	28	29	30	31

JUNE

S	M	T	W	T	F	S
1	2	3	4	5	6	7
8	9	10	11	12	13	14
15	16	17	18	19	20	21
22	23	24	25	26	27	28
29	30					

JULY

S	M	T	W	T	F	S
		1	2	3	4	5
6	7	8	9	10	11	12
13	14	15	16	17	18	19
20	21	22	23	24	25	26
27	28	29	30	31		

AUGUST

S	M	T	W	T	F	S
31					1	2
3	4	5	6	7	8	9
10	11	12	13	14	15	16
17	18	19	20	21	22	23
24	25	26	27	28	29	30

SEPTEMBER

S	M	T	W	T	F	S
	1	2	3	4	5	6
7	8	9	10	11	12	13
14	15	16	17	18	19	20
21	22	23	24	25	26	27
28	29	30				

OCTOBER

S	M	T	W	T	F	S
			1	2	3	4
5	6	7	8	9	10	11
12	13	14	15	16	17	18
19	20	21	22	23	24	25
26	27	28	29	30	31	

NOVEMBER

S	M	T	W	T	F	S
30						1
2	3	4	5	6	7	8
9	10	11	12	13	14	15
16	17	18	19	20	21	22
23	24	25	26	27	28	29

DECEMBER

S	M	T	W	T	F	S
	1	2	3	4	5	6
7	8	9	10	11	12	13
14	15	16	17	18	19	20
21	22	23	24	25	26	27
28	29	30	31			

2024

JANUARY
S	M	T	W	T	F	S
	1	2	3	4	5	6
7	8	9	10	11	12	13
14	15	16	17	18	19	20
21	22	23	24	25	26	27
28	29	30	31			

FEBRUARY
S	M	T	W	T	F	S
				1	2	3
4	5	6	7	8	9	10
11	12	13	14	15	16	17
18	19	20	21	22	23	24
25	26	27	28	29		

MARCH
S	M	T	W	T	F	S
31					1	2
3	4	5	6	7	8	9
10	11	12	13	14	15	16
17	18	19	20	21	22	23
24	25	26	27	28	29	30

APRIL
S	M	T	W	T	F	S
	1	2	3	4	5	6
7	8	9	10	11	12	13
14	15	16	17	18	19	20
21	22	23	24	25	26	27
28	29	30				

MAY
S	M	T	W	T	F	S
			1	2	3	4
5	6	7	8	9	10	11
12	13	14	15	16	17	18
19	20	21	22	23	24	25
26	27	28	29	30	31	

JUNE
S	M	T	W	T	F	S
30						1
2	3	4	5	6	7	8
9	10	11	12	13	14	15
16	17	18	19	20	21	22
23	24	25	26	27	28	29

JULY
S	M	T	W	T	F	S
	1	2	3	4	5	6
7	8	9	10	11	12	13
14	15	16	17	18	19	20
21	22	23	24	25	26	27
28	29	30	31			

AUGUST
S	M	T	W	T	F	S
				1	2	3
4	5	6	7	8	9	10
11	12	13	14	15	16	17
18	19	20	21	22	23	24
25	26	27	28	29	30	31

SEPTEMBER
S	M	T	W	T	F	S
1	2	3	4	5	6	7
8	9	10	11	12	13	14
15	16	17	18	19	20	21
22	23	24	25	26	27	28
29	30					

OCTOBER
S	M	T	W	T	F	S
		1	2	3	4	5
6	7	8	9	10	11	12
13	14	15	16	17	18	19
20	21	22	23	24	25	26
27	28	29	30	31		

NOVEMBER
S	M	T	W	T	F	S
					1	2
3	4	5	6	7	8	9
10	11	12	13	14	15	16
17	18	19	20	21	22	23
24	25	26	27	28	29	30

DECEMBER
S	M	T	W	T	F	S
1	2	3	4	5	6	7
8	9	10	11	12	13	14
15	16	17	18	19	20	21
22	23	24	25	26	27	28
29	30	31				

2026

JANUARY
S	M	T	W	T	F	S
				1	2	3
4	5	6	7	8	9	10
11	12	13	14	15	16	17
18	19	20	21	22	23	24
25	26	27	28	29	30	31

FEBRUARY
S	M	T	W	T	F	S
1	2	3	4	5	6	7
8	9	10	11	12	13	14
15	16	17	18	19	20	21
22	23	24	25	26	27	28

MARCH
S	M	T	W	T	F	S
1	2	3	4	5	6	7
8	9	10	11	12	13	14
15	16	17	18	19	20	21
22	23	24	25	26	27	28
29	30	31				

APRIL
S	M	T	W	T	F	S
			1	2	3	4
5	6	7	8	9	10	11
12	13	14	15	16	17	18
19	20	21	22	23	24	25
26	27	28	29	30		

MAY
S	M	T	W	T	F	S
31					1	2
3	4	5	6	7	8	9
10	11	12	13	14	15	16
17	18	19	20	21	22	23
24	25	26	27	28	29	30

JUNE
S	M	T	W	T	F	S
	1	2	3	4	5	6
7	8	9	10	11	12	13
14	15	16	17	18	19	20
21	22	23	24	25	26	27
28	29	30				

JULY
S	M	T	W	T	F	S
			1	2	3	4
5	6	7	8	9	10	11
12	13	14	15	16	17	18
19	20	21	22	23	24	25
26	27	28	29	30	31	

AUGUST
S	M	T	W	T	F	S
30	31					1
2	3	4	5	6	7	8
9	10	11	12	13	14	15
16	17	18	19	20	21	22
23	24	25	26	27	28	29

SEPTEMBER
S	M	T	W	T	F	S
		1	2	3	4	5
6	7	8	9	10	11	12
13	14	15	16	17	18	19
20	21	22	23	24	25	26
27	28	29	30			

OCTOBER
S	M	T	W	T	F	S
				1	2	3
4	5	6	7	8	9	10
11	12	13	14	15	16	17
18	19	20	21	22	23	24
25	26	27	28	29	30	31

NOVEMBER
S	M	T	W	T	F	S
1	2	3	4	5	6	7
8	9	10	11	12	13	14
15	16	17	18	19	20	21
22	23	24	25	26	27	28
29	30					

DECEMBER
S	M	T	W	T	F	S
		1	2	3	4	5
6	7	8	9	10	11	12
13	14	15	16	17	18	19
20	21	22	23	24	25	26
27	28	29	30	31		

Personal information

IF FOUND PLEASE CONTACT:

NAME

ADDRESS

STATE   POSTCODE

PHONE NUMBER   MOBILE

EMAIL

IN CASE OF EMERGENCY:

NAME

TELEPHONE   MOBILE

USEFUL TELEPHONE NUMBERS:

DOCTOR   GAS

DENTIST   ELECTRICITY

MECHANIC   WATER

VET   PLUMBER

CHILD CARE   SCHOOL

OTHER IMPORTANT INFORMATION:

Key contacts

NAME

ADDRESS

STATE   POSTCODE

TELEPHONE (H)   (W)

MOBILE   EMAIL

NAME

ADDRESS

STATE   POSTCODE

TELEPHONE (H)   (W)

MOBILE   EMAIL

NAME

ADDRESS

STATE   POSTCODE

TELEPHONE (H)   (W)

MOBILE   EMAIL

NAME

ADDRESS

STATE   POSTCODE

TELEPHONE (H)   (W)

MOBILE   EMAIL

NAME

ADDRESS

STATE   POSTCODE

TELEPHONE (H)   (W)

MOBILE   EMAIL

NAME

ADDRESS

STATE   POSTCODE

TELEPHONE (H)   (W)

MOBILE   EMAIL

Key contacts

NAME
....

ADDRESS
....

STATE   POSTCODE
....

TELEPHONE (H)   (W)
....

MOBILE   EMAIL
....

NAME
....

ADDRESS
....

STATE   POSTCODE
....

TELEPHONE (H)   (W)
....

MOBILE   EMAIL
....

NAME
....

ADDRESS
....

STATE   POSTCODE
....

TELEPHONE (H)   (W)
....

MOBILE   EMAIL
....

NAME
....

ADDRESS
....

STATE   POSTCODE
....

TELEPHONE (H)   (W)
....

MOBILE   EMAIL
....

NAME
....

ADDRESS
....

STATE   POSTCODE
....

TELEPHONE (H)   (W)
....

MOBILE   EMAIL
....

NAME
....

ADDRESS
....

STATE   POSTCODE
....

TELEPHONE (H)   (W)
....

MOBILE   EMAIL
....

Special events 2025

JANUARY

FEBRUARY

MARCH

APRIL

MAY

JUNE

JULY

AUGUST

SEPTEMBER

OCTOBER

NOVEMBER

DECEMBER

School terms 2025

NEW SOUTH WALES

TERM 1	January 31 – April 11
TERM 2	April 28 – July 4
TERM 3	July 21 – September 26
TERM 4	October 13 – December 19

AUSTRALIAN CAPITAL TERRITORY

TERM 1	January 31 – April 11
TERM 2	April 28 – July 4
TERM 3	July 21 – September 26
TERM 4	October 13 – December 18

QUEENSLAND

TERM 1	January 28 – April 4
TERM 2	April 22 – June 27
TERM 3	July 14 – September 19
TERM 4	October 7 – December 12

VICTORIA

TERM 1	January 28 – April 4
TERM 2	April 22 – July 4
TERM 3	July 21 – September 19
TERM 4	October 6 – December 19

WESTERN AUSTRALIA

TERM 1	February 5 – April 11
TERM 2	April 28 – July 4
TERM 3	July 21 – September 26
TERM 4	October 13 – December 18

NORTHERN TERRITORY

TERM 1	January 28 – April 4
TERM 2	April 14 – June 20
TERM 3	July 14 – September 19
TERM 4	October 6 – December 12

SOUTH AUSTRALIA

TERM 1	January 28 – April 11
TERM 2	April 28 – July 4
TERM 3	July 21 – September 26
TERM 4	October 13 – December 12

TASMANIA

TERM 1	February 3 – April 11
TERM 2	April 28 – July 4
TERM 3	July 21 – September 26
TERM 4	October 13 – December 19

CHECK WITH YOUR SCHOOL FOR DATES OF PUPIL-FREE DAYS

Budget planner 2025

For advice on how best to use this planner, see the Finance chapter in June.

$$$	WEEKLY	MONTHLY	ANNUALLY
INCOME			
Net salary/wage			
Bonuses (after tax)			
Dividends/income from investments			
Interest			
Other			
TOTAL INCOME			
EXPENDITURE			
HOUSEHOLD			
Rent/mortgage			
Council rates			
Water rates			
Power & heating			
Telephone/internet			
House & contents insurance			
Maintenance/repairs			
Other			
PERSONAL			
Groceries			
Clothing			
Child care			
School fees			
Toiletries/cosmetics/ haircare/massage			
Newspapers/magazines			
Superannuation			
Other			
LOANS			
Personal loans			
Credit/after pay			
Other			

$$$	WEEKLY	MONTHLY	ANNUALLY
TRANSPORT			
Public transport			
Car registration			
Car insurance			
Petrol			
Tolls			
Parking			
Other			
HEALTH			
Doctor/dentist/ other specialists			
Health insurance			
Chemist			
Life insurance/ income protection			
Other			
ENTERTAINMENT			
Eating out			
Concerts/movies/ theatre			
Memberships			
Holidays			
Hobbies			
Streaming services			
Other			
OTHER			
Gifts			
Donations to charity			
Regular investments			
Savings/rainy day fund			
TOTAL EXPENDITURE			
TOTAL INCOME			
INCOME MINUS EXPENDITURE			

DATE OF MY NEXT BUDGET REVIEW   /   /

Health checklist

	LOOKING FOR	HOW OFTEN
Eye examination	Vision loss, general eye health and conditions like glaucoma and cataracts.	Every 2-3 years from age 40 and yearly from age 65. More regularly if there is a family history of glaucoma, diabetes or high blood pressure.
Dental	Gum disease, cavities and general decline in dental health.	Once a year for a check-up and clean, or more often if you have gum issues or plaque build-up.
Hearing	Hearing loss.	When you notice hearing damage or have concerns, or annually for those aged 60 and over.
Bone density scan	Osteoporosis or low bone density.	Consult your GP if you are aged over 50 and have a high risk of osteoporosis.
Immunisation	Immunity to influenza, Covid-19, tetanus, rubella and others.	As advised by your GP. Flu shots are available yearly, and are free for those aged over 65.
Cervical Screening Test	Signs of the human papillomavirus (HPV) and cervical cancer.	From age 25-74 if you are or have ever been sexually active. If results are normal, continue to be tested every five years thereafter.
STI test	Common sexually transmitted diseases, such as chlamydia, gonorrhoea, syphilis, genital herpes, hepatitis B and HIV.	Every six to 12 months if you're sexually active, have a new partner, frequently change partners, travel to areas with a high prevalence of STIs or have been exposed in the last 12 months.
Breast self-examination	Breast changes, lumps, dimpling or thickening of the skin, nipple change or discharge, pain.	Know the normal look and feel of your breasts. If you notice any new or unusual changes, see your GP, particularly if they persist.
Screening mammogram	Breast lumps or changes not evident to the touch.	Every two years from age 50-74, or annually and earlier if at high risk of breast cancer.
Diabetes screening	Elevated blood glucose levels.	Screening is dependent on your individual risk level. Ask your GP for advice.
Skin check	Spots, moles and freckles which are dry, scaly or have smudgy borders.	Self-check on a regular basis and see your GP about any new or changed skin lesions. Get checked opportunistically if you work outdoors.
Bowel cancer screening	Polyps, other signs of bowel cancer.	Faecal occult blood test every two years from age 50-74, plus a five-yearly colonoscopy. Early testing is available for those deemed to be at moderate risk of bowel cancer; ask your GP.
Blood pressure	High blood pressure, which can increase risk of heart disease and stroke; low blood pressure.	Every two years for adults aged 18 and over, or more often if there's a family history of high blood pressure, stroke, kidney or heart disease.
Cholesterol	High LDL (bad cholesterol) and triglycerides, and low HDL (good cholesterol).	Every five years from age 45, or more often if you're at risk of cardiovascular disease. The results, along with your BP results, will be interpreted by your GP in the context of your overall absolute cardiovascular risk.
Body Mass Index	Healthy weight range and waist measurement.	Every two years by your GP or more if part of an identified or increased risk group.

LAST CHECKED	CONTACT	DATE OF APPOINTMENT	COMPLETED
	For more information, visit health.gov.au/ncsp or call 1800 627 701		
	BreastScreen Australia: 132 050		
	For more information, visit health.gov.au/nbcsp or call 1800 627 701		

Aboriginal and Torres Strait Islander people may have different health needs; discuss these with your doctor.

Don't forget

WHY I SUPPORT BREAST CANCER TRIALS

I'm deeply thankful for the lifesaving treatment I received 10 years ago. I struggle to remember things, and insomnia, joint pain and nerve damage are part of every day for me. I'm hopeful research will find kinder treatments so others don't have to suffer after breast cancer.

Naveena Nekkalapudi, diagnosed age 39

let's talk about
HEALTHY HABITS

As we begin a new year, now's the perfect time to reflect on your health achievements over the last year and identify opportunities for growth and positive change in the months ahead.

While many Australians will take the opportunity to set some New Year's resolutions at the start of 2025, statistics predict that more than half will be unable to see them through. Often this can be due to a lack of planning or choosing goals that are unachievable. Set yourself up for a successful 2025 by working through the following steps.

1 DO A REVIEW OF 2024
Reflect on the year that was, including any achievements or challenges along the way. What worked well and what didn't? Did you meet your goals last year and if not, what stopped you? Use any setbacks and failures as a learning opportunity, and be sure to celebrate the small wins, whether that was exercising more, reducing your coffee intake or learning a new skill.

2 SET REASONABLE GOALS
Based on last year's learnings, put together a draft list of what you'd like to achieve in the next 12 months. Your goals might be diet or exercise-based, or social, emotional or financial aspirations. Aim for goals that are sustainable, specific and that tie in with your core values. Allow some flexibility so you don't give up at the first hurdle. Now choose one goal to start with rather than spreading yourself too thin between multiple objectives.

3 DO YOUR PREP WORK
Put systems in place to support your goal, whether that's sourcing new equipment, downloading apps or doing research. Seek outside support, enlist an accountability buddy or share your intentions with friends and family so they can help motivate you along the way.

4 START WITH SMALL STEPS
Most goals can't be reached overnight, and expecting too much too soon can set you up for failure. Instead, break each goal into measurable steps. For example, if your goal is to run five kilometres non-stop, ease yourself into it by perhaps aiming for two interval runs (swapping between walking and running) per week until your fitness improves. If your goal is to reduce stress, try meditating on alternate mornings. Track your progress in an app or notebook, and reward each step as you achieve it.

MY 2025 GOALS	MY PREP WORK	MY STEPS
1.		
2.		
3.		

5 ADAPT AS NEEDED

If, after a few months, you find that motivation is lagging or you haven't made the progress you'd hoped to, take some time to reevaluate your strategies, remind yourself of your why and tweak your plan. Most importantly, don't give up.

WHAT'S NOT WORKING?	TWEAKS

DECEMBER						
S	M	T	W	T	F	S
1	2	3	4	5	6	7
8	9	10	11	12	13	14
15	16	17	18	19	20	21
22	23	24	25	26	27	28
29	30	31				

JANUARY						
S	M	T	W	T	F	S
			1	2	3	4
5	6	7	8	9	10	11
12	13	14	15	16	17	18
19	20	21	22	23	24	25
26	27	28	29	30	31	

FEBRUARY						
S	M	T	W	T	F	S
						1
2	3	4	5	6	7	8
9	10	11	12	13	14	15
16	17	18	19	20	21	22
23	24	25	26	27	28	

30 MONDAY

31 TUESDAY NEW YEAR'S EVE

1 WEDNESDAY NEW YEAR'S DAY

2 THURSDAY

January
2025

3 FRIDAY

4 SATURDAY

5 SUNDAY

DECEMBER						
S	M	T	W	T	F	S
1	2	3	4	5	6	7
8	9	10	11	12	13	14
15	16	17	18	19	20	21
22	23	24	25	26	27	28
29	30	31				

JANUARY						
S	M	T	W	T	F	S
			1	2	3	4
5	6	7	8	9	10	11
12	13	14	15	16	17	18
19	20	21	22	23	24	25
26	27	28	29	30	31	

FEBRUARY						
S	M	T	W	T	F	S
						1
2	3	4	5	6	7	8
9	10	11	12	13	14	15
16	17	18	19	20	21	22
23	24	25	26	27	28	

6 MONDAY

7 TUESDAY

8 WEDNESDAY

9 THURSDAY

January
2025

10 FRIDAY

11 SATURDAY

PRIORITISE YOUR GUT HEALTH THIS YEAR. Add more fibre-rich, plant-based foods to your diet to boost the digestive system and reduce heartburn, bloating and constipation.

12 SUNDAY

DECEMBER

S	M	T	W	T	F	S
1	2	3	4	5	6	7
8	9	10	11	12	13	14
15	16	17	18	19	20	21
22	23	24	25	26	27	28
29	30	31				

JANUARY

S	M	T	W	T	F	S
			1	2	3	4
5	6	7	8	9	10	11
12	13	14	15	16	17	18
19	20	21	22	23	24	25
26	27	28	29	30	31	

FEBRUARY

S	M	T	W	T	F	S
						1
2	3	4	5	6	7	8
9	10	11	12	13	14	15
16	17	18	19	20	21	22
23	24	25	26	27	28	

13 MONDAY

14 TUESDAY

15 WEDNESDAY

16 THURSDAY

17 FRIDAY

18 SATURDAY

SIGN UP FOR OUR DOG WALK CHALLENGE held during February to kickstart your fitness goals. Go walkies to save lives! Visit breastcancertrials.org.au/fundraise.

19 SUNDAY

DECEMBER						
S	M	T	W	T	F	S
1	2	3	4	5	6	7
8	9	10	11	12	13	14
15	16	17	18	19	20	21
22	23	24	25	26	27	28
29	30	31				

JANUARY						
S	M	T	W	T	F	S
			1	2	3	4
5	6	7	8	9	10	11
12	13	14	15	16	17	18
19	20	21	22	23	24	25
26	27	28	29	30	31	

FEBRUARY						
S	M	T	W	T	F	S
						1
2	3	4	5	6	7	8
9	10	11	12	13	14	15
16	17	18	19	20	21	22
23	24	25	26	27	28	

20 MONDAY

21 TUESDAY

22 WEDNESDAY

23 THURSDAY

January 2025

24 FRIDAY

25 SATURDAY

MAKE TIME FOR A DIGITAL SECURITY AUDIT. Change your PINs and passwords, renew antivirus software and update ICE (In Case of Emergency) contacts in your phone.

26 SUNDAY AUSTRALIA DAY

	DECEMBER					
S	M	T	W	T	F	S
1	2	3	4	5	6	7
8	9	10	11	12	13	14
15	16	17	18	19	20	21
22	23	24	25	26	27	28
29	30	31				

	JANUARY					
S	M	T	W	T	F	S
				1	2	3	4
5	6	7	8	9	10	11
12	13	14	15	16	17	18
19	20	21	22	23	24	25
26	27	28	29	30	31	

	FEBRUARY					
S	M	T	W	T	F	S
						1
2	3	4	5	6	7	8
9	10	11	12	13	14	15
16	17	18	19	20	21	22
23	24	25	26	27	28	

27 MONDAY AUSTRALIA DAY PUBLIC HOLIDAY, ISRA AND MI'RAJ (ISLAMIC HOLY DAY)

28 TUESDAY

29 WEDNESDAY LUNAR NEW YEAR

30 THURSDAY

January – February 2025

31 FRIDAY

1 SATURDAY

2 SUNDAY

WHY I SUPPORT BREAST CANCER TRIALS

I found the lump myself and was shocked when it was breast cancer. Our boys were just 4, 7 and 13, and after a big cry, my husband and I made a deal to do everything we could to beat it. Since then, four people I know have been diagnosed, too. I encourage everyone to be vigilant and have regular screening.

**Belinda Ward,
diagnosed age 45,
pictured with her family**

let's talk about
BEING ACTIVE

No matter how old you are, moving your body every day can have a positive impact on all areas of your health. Find ways to make physical activity a regular part of your lifestyle to reap the rewards.

When it comes to exercise, variety is key. Enjoying a range of activities will ensure that we don't get bored, hit a plateau or overwork or neglect certain muscle groups. And as the seasons change and temperatures fluctuate (along with our motivation), it makes sense that we tailor our choices to the weather conditions. Use this seasonal guide to tick off a range of exercise options. It will also help you to meet the current Australian physical activity and sedentary behaviour guidelines for adults aged 18-64 years, which call for a combination of moderate- and vigorous-intensity activity, along with exercises that build muscle strength.

SUMMER	AUTUMN	WINTER	SPRING
Avoid peak temperatures by exercising first thing in the morning or later in the day. Look for water-based activities or those that can be done in air-conditioning. Wear light clothing and stay hydrated!	Enjoy the milder temperatures and embrace the changing scenery with outdoor activities. It's a good time of year to train for an event, like a fun run or triathlon, or take a guided walk in nature.	Motivation can be hard to find on cold days. Try wearing workout clothes to bed so you're ready to go first thing, or exercise in your lunch break. Indoor classes or home-based workouts are great on chilly days.	Spring symbolises a fresh start – take this opportunity to try a new activity or team sport. If you suffer from hay fever, avoid outdoor exercise when pollen counts are high – usually early morning and early evening.
BONUS TIP Many gyms will offer membership discounts to coincide with the new year – take advantage.	Raking leaves and planting bulbs for spring are both excellent forms of incidental exercise.	Do laps of the local shopping centre or climb the stairs at work for an efficient indoor workout.	Spring cleaning your house is the ultimate form of exercise, moving your body in myriad ways.
TRY Water aerobics, Pilates, walking, gym classes, kayaking, table tennis.	Cycling, jogging, bush walks, soccer, geocaching, yoga, golf, tennis.	Skiing, squash, home workouts, dancing, indoor swimming, rock climbing.	Outdoor yoga, netball, paddleboarding, martial arts, lawn bowls, gardening.

For more information, visit Exercise Right; exerciseright.com.au

Common exercise myths busted

Regular physical activity brings a number of health benefits. It can boost our mood and wellbeing, assist with weight loss and help reduce the risk of health conditions, such as type 2 diabetes, heart disease and some cancers. Yet some misconceptions around fitness could prevent us from enjoying our recommended 30 minutes each day. Here we discredit those myths.

MYTH: I need to take 10,000 steps a day The number 10,000 was devised by a pedometer manufacturer in the 1960s, and more recent research suggests women who get 4400 steps a day have lower mortality rates than those leading more sedentary lifestyles. In simple terms, aim to do a little more than what you do currently.

MYTH: Women shouldn't lift weights It's commonly thought that lifting weights can make women look too 'bulky' and muscular, but in fact, it's recommended we incorporate at least two 20-minute strength sessions into each week to help tone and strengthen our bodies. Lifting light weights can also improve our metabolism and increase bone density.

MYTH: You need to do 30 minutes in one lump sum Any activity is better than none, so don't be discouraged if you can't find a full 30 minutes in your schedule to exercise. Break it into three lots of 10 minutes and build incidental exercise into your day – walk to the shops, work in the garden or jump on the trampoline with the kids.

MYTH: You shouldn't exercise while pregnant For low-risk pregnancies, gentle exercise is encouraged until birth to reduce the risk of gestational diabetes, aid labour and recovery, strengthen the pelvic floor and manage anxiety and depression. Some modifications will be needed. Seek advice from your GP or an exercise physiologist.

MYTH: I'm too old to exercise Many older Australians believe that they're too weak or frail to exercise. But being physically active on most if not all days is especially important as we get older, helping to enhance muscle tone, increase bone density and improve balance and flexibility. Seek advice from your doctor to find an option that is suitable for you.

3 reasons why group exercise is good for you

Exercising as part of a group comes with many benefits, from boosting mental wellbeing to creating connections and providing an economic alternative to some solo activities. Most importantly, it helps make exercise enjoyable. Read up on the benefits, then find an option that appeals.

1 It's a great social opportunity

Joining an exercise class or group in your local area can help you meet like-minded people with similar goals and interests. This can then create opportunities to carpool to classes or games, meet for coffee before or after your activity or organise social gatherings outside of your workouts. You can also enlist an existing friend to join the activity with you, creating a standard diary date for catch-ups.

2 Your exercise quality is often better

When you exercise on your own, you're more likely to be inconsistent or get bored after a while. But exercising with other people can motivate you to exercise for longer, at a faster pace or to try something new. The collective energy that you find in a group setting is often contagious, helping to boost your enjoyment and push you to do better.

3 You're more likely to stick with it

The advantage of this type of exercise is that it usually takes place at a set time and place, so it can quickly become a part of your routine. Knowing that others are expecting you, especially in the case of team sports, makes you more compelled to show up and participate.

Simple resistance exercises to try at home

Resistance training, also known as strength training, can help us maintain a healthy weight, improve our balance and reduce our risk of depression and other mental health disorders. It's also been found to reduce the severity of some menopausal symptoms, increase bone density and improve sleep.

Resistance training uses weights or other resistance aids, such as weight machines, resistance bands and our own body weight, to increase muscle strength and endurance. Aim for two or three 30-minute sessions each week, made up of a range of exercises targeting different muscle groups (arms, legs, torso). Seek advice from an exercise professional first, to tailor a program to your needs and ensure the right technique. Exercises might include the following:

STANDING WALL PUSH-UP
TARGETS: Chest and shoulders

Stand with feet shoulder-width apart. Lean against the wall with arms outstretched. Lift your heels off the floor and, keeping your body straight, let your chest move towards the wall, then push back with your arms. Aim for two sets of 8-10 push-ups.

BICEP CURLS
TARGETS: Arms

Stand tall with feet hip-width apart. Hold a light dumbbell in each hand (tinned tomatoes also work) and relax arms by sides, palms facing forward. Engage the abdominals and bend at the elbow to lift weights to your shoulders. Keep elbows tucked in close to the body and upper arms stable. Lower weights to starting position; aim for three sets of 10.

PELVIC LIFT
TARGETS: Core and glutes

Lie on your back and bend your knees so feet are flat and hip-width apart. Squeeze the muscles in your abdomen and buttocks, then lift your hips so your shoulders, hips and knees are in a straight line. Hold for several seconds, relax the muscles and lower back down. Repeat.

CHAIR SITS
TARGETS: Legs and balance

Sit towards the middle or front of a chair with hands on your knees. Breathe out as you stand up, using your hands on your knees for assistance if you need to. Keep your back straight as you stand up in one movement. Lower yourself back down into the chair in a controlled movement – don't drop into the chair. Repeat.

WE NEED YOUR FEEDBACK

Help us to keep in touch with what matters to you and ensure your diary remains relevant, practical and informative by completing our short online survey today.

You can also unlock special offers like pre-ordering your 2026 Australian Women's Health Diary at a discounted price!

SCAN THIS CODE OR GO TO
breastcancertrials.org.au/
VIPdiaryoffer

2 MINUTES IS ALL YOU NEED!

BREAST CANCER TRIALS

	JANUARY							FEBRUARY							MARCH					
S	M	T	W	T	F	S	S	M	T	W	T	F	S	S	M	T	W	T	F	S
			1	2	3	4							1	30	31					1
5	6	7	8	9	10	11	2	3	4	5	6	7	8	2	3	4	5	6	7	8
12	13	14	15	16	17	18	9	10	11	12	13	14	15	9	10	11	12	13	14	15
19	20	21	22	23	24	25	16	17	18	19	20	21	22	16	17	18	19	20	21	22
26	27	28	29	30	31		23	24	25	26	27	28		23	24	25	26	27	28	29

3 MONDAY

4 TUESDAY

5 WEDNESDAY

6 THURSDAY

February
2025

7 FRIDAY

8 SATURDAY

IF YOU'RE OVER 40, have a chronic illness or have been sedentary for some time, see your doctor before starting a new exercise routine.

9 SUNDAY

		J A N U A R Y							F E B R U A R Y							M A R C H				
S	M	T	W	T	F	S	S	M	T	W	T	F	S	S	M	T	W	T	F	S
				1	2	3	4						1	30	31					1
5	6	7	8	9	10	11	2	3	4	5	6	7	8	2	3	4	5	6	7	8
12	13	14	15	16	17	18	9	10	11	12	13	14	15	9	10	11	12	13	14	15
19	20	21	22	23	24	25	16	17	18	19	20	21	22	16	17	18	19	20	21	22
26	27	28	29	30	31		23	24	25	26	27	28		23	24	25	26	27	28	29

10 MONDAY ROYAL HOBART REGATTA (TAS)

11 TUESDAY

12 WEDNESDAY

13 THURSDAY

14 FRIDAY   VALENTINE'S DAY

15 SATURDAY

16 SUNDAY

CLEANING THE HOUSE and working in the garden are both excellent forms of strength training. Think bending, pushing, lifting, digging and scrubbing.

JANUARY						
S	M	T	W	T	F	S
			1	2	3	4
5	6	7	8	9	10	11
12	13	14	15	16	17	18
19	20	21	22	23	24	25
26	27	28	29	30	31	

FEBRUARY						
S	M	T	W	T	F	S
						1
2	3	4	5	6	7	8
9	10	11	12	13	14	15
16	17	18	19	20	21	22
23	24	25	26	27	28	

MARCH						
S	M	T	W	T	F	S
30	31					1
2	3	4	5	6	7	8
9	10	11	12	13	14	15
16	17	18	19	20	21	22
23	24	25	26	27	28	29

17 MONDAY

18 TUESDAY

19 WEDNESDAY

20 THURSDAY

February 2025

21 FRIDAY

22 SATURDAY

CARE FOR THE ENVIRONMENT while exercising with plogging or plalking – a new sustainable initiative that combines jogging or walking with picking up litter.

23 SUNDAY

JANUARY						
S	M	T	W	T	F	S
			1	2	3	4
5	6	7	8	9	10	11
12	13	14	15	16	17	18
19	20	21	22	23	24	25
26	27	28	29	30	31	

FEBRUARY						
S	M	T	W	T	F	S
						1
2	3	4	5	6	7	8
9	10	11	12	13	14	15
16	17	18	19	20	21	22
23	24	25	26	27	28	

MARCH						
S	M	T	W	T	F	S
30	31					1
2	3	4	5	6	7	8
9	10	11	12	13	14	15
16	17	18	19	20	21	22
23	24	25	26	27	28	29

24 MONDAY

25 TUESDAY

26 WEDNESDAY

27 THURSDAY

February – March
2025

28 FRIDAY

1 SATURDAY RAMADAN BEGINS

IF MOTIVATION IS LACKING, get more enjoyment out of exercise by listening to music (uptempo is best), your favourite podcast or an audiobook while you do it.

2 SUNDAY

"

I worked in an oncology clinic where I saw the impact of breast cancer and learned about the role of clinical trials. I remember when Herceptin was discovered, and I didn't know how much this treatment would mean to me personally until I was diagnosed. I am now on Letrozole, also thanks to clinical trials.

Kim Reed, diagnosed age 52, pictured with her husband and pet dog

let's talk about
NUTRITION

Following a healthy diet can prove difficult when time constraints, rising grocery costs and other health factors come into play. Make informed choices with guidance from this chapter.

Not all processed foods are created equal. While some are an essential part of a healthy diet, others contain nasty additives and have minimal nutritional value. Here, we explain the difference, to help you strike the right balance.

1 MINIMALLY PROCESSED FOODS
Examples: Roasted nuts, pre-packaged salad mix, frozen fruit. These foods are slightly changed from their natural state – for example, frozen, dried, fermented, vacuum-sealed or roasted. These alterations do not diminish the foods' health benefits, and often make them easier to find and consume.

2 PROCESSED INGREDIENTS
Examples: Cold pressed olive oil, milled flour, refined sugar. These common cooking ingredients come from natural sources that are slightly altered to make them easier to use. They're not usually eaten alone, but are added during cooking.

3 PROCESSED FOODS
Examples: Dried pasta, some types of bread, canned fish, tofu, cheese. Generally foods from the first two groups that have added salt, sugar, fat and other additives to enhance their taste, lengthen their shelf life or reduce their preparation time.

4 ULTRA-PROCESSED FOODS (UPFS)
Examples: Packaged biscuits, chips, soft drinks, lollies, alcohol. These foods have undergone intense manufacturing processes, which strip them of their basic nutritional benefits. They typically contain chemicals, such as preservatives, colours, flavours and artificial sweeteners. Studies show that regular UPF consumption can increase our risk of chronic diseases such as type 2 diabetes, cardiovascular disease, depression and many cancers. For this reason, Australian dietary guidelines recommend limiting our intake of these foods to only sometimes and in small amounts.

HOW TO STRIKE THE RIGHT BALANCE
While whole foods and minimally processed options are ideal from a nutrition perspective, processed foods bring convenience to our busy lives, with lots of healthy options among the not-so-healthy, such as wholegrain bread, low-fat milk, canned legumes, frozen fruits and cereals fortified with vitamins. Always refer to the nutrition label on packaged foods. The more ingredients, the more processing involved, the more they should be avoided.

For more information, visit Nutrition Australia; nutritionaustralia.org

Healthy meal planning

Whether you're cooking for one or for the whole family, meal planning is an effective way to eat well on a budget while still ensuring your daily nutritional needs are met. Planning out your meals in advance allows you to use ingredients that you already have, saves time and mental energy, reduces food waste, helps you to be more intentional with your spending and lessens the temptation to order unhealthy takeaway. Follow these steps to make meal planning work for you.

Plan around what you have

Do an audit of your fridge, freezer and pantry and plan meals based on what's already on hand. Aim to use up any fresh produce or items that are near their use-by date first, to reduce food waste and save money on your grocery spend for that period.

Shop smart

Buy fruit and vegetables when they're in season – they'll be fresher and more economical. And don't discount canned and frozen fruit and vegetables, which still offer plenty of nutritional benefits along with a longer shelf life.

Use ingredients in multiple ways

This will help reduce waste. For example, if you're buying a head of lettuce, use it on sandwiches one day, in a salad the next day and as lettuce cups later in the week.

Embrace batch cooking

Make double or triple quantities of your meals, which can then be frozen or reheated for lunch the next day or later in the week. Think soups, casseroles and stir-fries. There's also nothing wrong with having the same healthy breakfast every day, and it's a great way to use things up.

Cover off the five food groups

To meet your daily dietary requirements, plan meals that include grains, fruit and/or vegetables, some form of protein or dairy/a dairy alternative. You don't need to include all food groups in each meal – just aim for a good mix across the day. Use the check list (below) to keep track.

TICK OFF YOUR DAILY DIETARY REQUIREMENTS (FOR ADULTS)

☐ **5 serves of vegetables**

☐ **2 serves of fruit**

☐ **6 serves of grains**
4 serves after age 50; 3 serves after age 70; 8-9 serves if pregnant or breastfeeding

☐ **2½ serves of lean meat, fish, poultry, eggs, nuts, seeds, legumes and beans**
2 serves after age 50; 3½-4 serves if pregnant or breastfeeding

☐ **2½ serves of milk, yoghurt, cheese and non-dairy alternatives**
4 serves after age 50; 3½-4 serves if pregnant or breastfeeding

CHOOSE SIMPLE MEALS THAT USE MINIMAL INGREDIENTS
There's no need to serve Michelin star-worthy meals each day. When inspiration is lacking, choose two to three favourite lunches and some tried and tested dinners to see you through.

SAMPLE MEAL PLANNER

	BREAKFAST	LUNCH	DINNER	SNACKS
S				
M				
T				
W				
T				
F				
S				

INGREDIENTS I ALREADY HAVE	INGREDIENTS I NEED TO BUY

Spotlight on caffeine

Around 27 per cent of Australians claim they can't get through the day without coffee, and while research suggests caffeine has some health benefits, overconsumption can cause negative side effects.

WHAT IS CAFFEINE? Caffeine is a natural stimulant found in coffee, black and green tea, chocolate, cola and energy drinks. Once consumed, caffeine is absorbed into the blood stream, travelling to the brain and central nervous system to help us feel awake and alert.

THE UPSIDES In moderate doses, caffeine can improve mood and help us feel alert and focused. Polyphenols (plant compounds) in caffeine have anti-inflammatory and antioxidant benefits, and drinking coffee may lower the risk of type 2 diabetes, be beneficial for liver disease and reduce the risk of certain types of cancer. Coffee may also improve some symptoms of Parkinson's disease and lower the risk of Alzheimer's disease and depression.

THE DOWNSIDES In large doses (more than the recommended 400 milligrams or 3-4 cups per day), caffeine can contribute to feelings of anxiety, irritability and may cause dizziness or headaches. It can also affect sleep. Over time you can become dependent on caffeine and may experience withdrawal symptoms (fatigue, headaches, sweating, muscle pain) if you suddenly stop drinking it.

ADDITIONAL GUIDELINES It's advised that children, people with high blood pressure and the elderly take care with caffeine. Pregnant women should limit their intake to 200mg (1-2 cups) per day.

APPROXIMATE CAFFEINE CONTENTS OF EVERYDAY FOOD AND DRINKS	
Chocolate drinks	5-10mg per 250ml
Instant coffee	80-120mg per 250ml
Drip/percolated coffee	150-240mg per 250ml
Espresso coffee	105-110mg per 250ml
Decaffeinated coffee	2-6mg per 250ml
Black tea	65-105mg per 250ml
Green tea	25-45mg per 250ml
Cola drinks	36mg per 375ml
Energy drinks	80mg per 250 ml
Dark chocolate bar	40-50mg per 55g
Milk chocolate bar	10mg per 50g
Matcha	60-75mg per 250ml

6 reasons NOT to count calories

Many weight-loss programs follow a "calories in, calories out" philosophy, also known as calorie counting. The idea is that eating a calorie-controlled diet can help you drop a few kilos, particularly when combined with exercise. However, many health professionals advise against this approach, recommending that we focus on the nutritional value of the foods we eat, rather than the number of calories they contain. Here are six reasons to avoid calorie counting.

1 It's not an exact science
It's difficult to determine how many calories (or kilojoules) a person should consume, with age, gender, weight, height, metabolic rate and physical activity all coming into play. Not to mention, the calories listed on food packets are only estimates with discrepancies of up to 20 per cent.

2 It's time consuming
While packaged foods list the estimated number of calories per serve, whole foods don't come with labels, so the onus is on you to weigh and measure everything you eat and then accurately input the data into an app or calorie calculator. Doing this multiple times a day can become tedious.

3 The mental toll
The rigid nature of this dieting strategy goes against our body's biological needs. In addition, opting for low-calorie options or tiny portions can leave you feeling deprived, increase feelings of anxiety or guilt around eating and may lead to disordered eating or binge eating.

4 Nutrition takes a back seat
Focusing on calorie content can mean you're missing out on vital nutrients that assist with weight loss, such as protein, fibre, good carbs and fats. This can lead to fatigue, low energy levels and slow the metabolism, making it difficult to maintain weight loss.

5 Social eating becomes difficult
Calculating calories while eating out, when portions are unknown, can lead to anxiety and cause you to avoid social occasions altogether. This can then contribute to isolation and depression.

6 We lose touch with our bodies
Eating foods based on the number attached to them can reduce our ability to recognise hunger and fullness cues. We might skip meals due to calories consumed or overeat past a comfortably full stage.

F E B R U A R Y						
S	M	T	W	T	F	S
						1
2	3	4	5	6	7	8
9	10	11	12	13	14	15
16	17	18	19	20	21	22
23	24	25	26	27	28	

M A R C H						
S	M	T	W	T	F	S
30	31					1
2	3	4	5	6	7	8
9	10	11	12	13	14	15
16	17	18	19	20	21	22
23	24	25	26	27	28	29

A P R I L						
S	M	T	W	T	F	S
		1	2	3	4	5
6	7	8	9	10	11	12
13	14	15	16	17	18	19
20	21	22	23	24	25	26
27	28	29	30			

3 MONDAY LABOUR DAY (WA)

4 TUESDAY

5 WEDNESDAY ASH WEDNESDAY, LENT BEGINS

6 THURSDAY

March
2025

7 FRIDAY

8 SATURDAY INTERNATIONAL WOMEN'S DAY

9 SUNDAY

		FEBRUARY							MARCH							APRIL			
S	M	T	W	T	F	S	S	M	T	W	T	F	S	S	M	T	W	T	F	S
						1	30	31					1				1	2	3	4	5
2	3	4	5	6	7	8	2	3	4	5	6	7	8	6	7	8	9	10	11	12
9	10	11	12	13	14	15	9	10	11	12	13	14	15	13	14	15	16	17	18	19
16	17	18	19	20	21	22	16	17	18	19	20	21	22	20	21	22	23	24	25	26
23	24	25	26	27	28		23	24	25	26	27	28	29	27	28	29	30			

10 MONDAY LABOUR DAY (VIC), EIGHT HOURS DAY (TAS), ADELAIDE CUP (SA), CANBERRA DAY (ACT)

11 TUESDAY

12 WEDNESDAY

13 THURSDAY

March
2025

14 FRIDAY

15 SATURDAY

AVOID THE TEMPTATION of sweet treats and ultra-processed foods when grocery shopping by sticking to the outer aisles only or doing your shopping online.

16 SUNDAY

		FEBRUARY								MARCH								APRIL			
S	M	T	W	T	F	S		S	M	T	W	T	F	S		S	M	T	W	T	F	S
						1		30	31					1				1	2	3	4	5
2	3	4	5	6	7	8		2	3	4	5	6	7	8		6	7	8	9	10	11	12
9	10	11	12	13	14	15		9	10	11	12	13	14	15		13	14	15	16	17	18	19
16	17	18	19	20	21	22		16	17	18	19	20	21	22		20	21	22	23	24	25	26
23	24	25	26	27	28			23	24	25	26	27	28	29		27	28	29	30			

17 MONDAY ST PATRICK'S DAY

18 TUESDAY

19 WEDNESDAY

20 THURSDAY NATIONAL CLOSE THE GAP DAY, NOWRUZ (PERSIAN NEW YEAR)

March
2025

21 FRIDAY   HARMONY DAY

22 SATURDAY

23 SUNDAY

FEBRUARY						
S	M	T	W	T	F	S
						1
2	3	4	5	6	7	8
9	10	11	12	13	14	15
16	17	18	19	20	21	22
23	24	25	26	27	28	

MARCH						
S	M	T	W	T	F	S
30	31					1
2	3	4	5	6	7	8
9	10	11	12	13	14	15
16	17	18	19	20	21	22
23	24	25	26	27	28	29

APRIL						
S	M	T	W	T	F	S
		1	2	3	4	5
6	7	8	9	10	11	12
13	14	15	16	17	18	19
20	21	22	23	24	25	26
27	28	29	30			

24 MONDAY

25 TUESDAY

26 WEDNESDAY

27 THURSDAY

March
2025

28 FRIDAY

29 SATURDAY

> **ADD MORE PLANT FOODS TO YOUR PLATE** for ample health benefits. Blend up a green smoothie, add lentils to bolognese or make hearty salads your main meal.

30 SUNDAY

WHY I SUPPORT BREAST CANCER TRIALS

It's very challenging for me to not worry for the future, but I try to really enjo
moments with my family and be hopeful that with all the trials, including th
one I am participating in for early-stage disease, there might be a cure.

Laura Yang, diagnosed age 39

let's talk about
WOMEN'S HEALTH

When it comes to navigating and preventing the range of health conditions that specifically affect women at all stages of life, knowledge is your most powerful tool.

Polycystic ovary syndrome (PCOS) is a hormonal condition that affects one in eight women. Most are not aware they have it. PCOS can cause short and long-term health problems, affecting fertility and posing a risk during pregnancy and bringing an increased risk of diabetes, heart disease and some mental health challenges. Until recently, PCOS was often undiagnosed, under-researched and misunderstood, however, recent updates to guidelines around diagnosis, support and treatment are hoping to change this.

SYMPTOMS OF PCOS

Women may experience varying symptoms ranging from mild to severe, including:

- Irregular or absent periods
- Periods with heavy or light bleeding
- Excess body and facial hair
- Hair loss or thinning around the scalp
- Acne or skin tags
- Difficulties falling pregnant
- Weight gain, often around the mid-section.

In addition to these physical symptoms, women may also experience low self-esteem and body image, feel anxious or depressed or suffer from disordered eating associated with weight gain. There's also a higher risk of diabetes and heart disease.

CAUSES

The cause of PCOS is unknown, however, having a close family member with PCOS is thought to increase your chances of having it by 50 per cent. Lifestyle can make the symptoms of PCOS better or worse. Increased levels of insulin in the body can also cause many of the complications of PCOS, such as irregular periods, hair and skin conditions and ovulation issues.

DIAGNOSIS AND TREATMENT

See your GP if you experience any of the above symptoms. They may order an ultrasound or blood test to check hormone levels and look for follicular abnormalities. If diagnosed, targeted treatments can address the symptoms. For example, laser therapy to control excess body hair or the oral contraceptive pill to improve acne and regulate menstrual cycles. A healthy lifestyle can also reduce the symptoms – eat a balanced diet, enjoy regular exercise and cease harmful habits like smoking and excessive drinking.

For more information, visit AskPCOS; askpcos.org.

5 important health questions to ask your parents

Some health conditions can be passed down through families, including heart disease, mental illness, diabetes, dementia and some cancers. So, if possible, it can be helpful to ask your mum, dad or other blood relatives about their medical history, and share this information with your doctor and your own children. A familial risk does not guarantee you'll also have it, but having this information puts you in a better position to reduce your risk. Ask these questions.

1 **"Has anyone in our family had cancer?"** Most cancers occur without previous family links. However, some cancers (up to five per cent), including breast, ovarian, melanoma and bowel, carry an increased risk when a faulty gene exists. Knowing which of your blood relatives have had cancer and their age when they had it can help pinpoint this familial risk, and give you access to family counselling services to discuss your options for screening and risk-reduction strategies moving forward.

2 **"How is your heart health?"** If there is a history of high blood pressure, diabetes, high cholesterol, heart attack or stroke among your immediate family, you should flag this with your GP to monitor your own risk of developing these conditions. Lifestyle factors, such as poor diet, smoking and lack of physical activity, can also elevate your risk, but unlike your genes, you can change these factors.

3 **"Mum, what was your pregnancy like?"** Your chance of developing certain fertility-impacting conditions, such as endometriosis and polycystic ovary syndrome (PCOS), is greater if one of your female blood relatives experienced it. Likewise, other complications, such as stillbirth, miscarriage, gestational diabetes, preeclampsia and premature birth, can all have links with familial history and be managed by your doctor.

4 **"When did you go through menopause?"** Your final menstrual period is likely to happen at a similar time to your mother's. It's particularly important if your mum experienced non-medically induced premature menopause (before the age of 40), which can affect your fertility and put you at a higher risk of osteoporosis and cardiovascular disease.

5 **"Have you ever suffered from a mental health disorder?"** Mental health conditions and disorders, including anxiety, depression, postnatal depression, bipolar disorder and schizophrenia, can run in families. This doesn't guarantee you'll experience the same thing, and your own life events and lifestyle choices (drug and alcohol use, physical activity, social supports) can play a key role. Bear in mind that society's attitudes to mental health have changed over time, and your parents may not have had a formal diagnosis or may use different terminology.

For more information, visit Jean Hailes for Women's Health; jeanhailes.org.au

What is pelvic floor dysfunction?

Hidden from view between the coccyx (tailbone) and the pubic bone within the pelvis, our pelvic floor muscles work hard to tighten and relax as needed to support the bowel, bladder, uterus and vagina. If these muscles become weakened, such as from pregnancy, childbirth, chronic constipation, obesity or getting older, you may find it more difficult to control your urine, faeces or wind. If you've ever accidentally passed wind, felt a little urine leak out when you coughed, laughed or jumped, experienced pain during sex or felt a constant need to go to the toilet, these may be signs of pelvic floor dysfunction. Try these steps to address it:

● Seek help from a pelvic floor physiotherapist, GP or continence specialist, who can discuss the best treatment for your needs.

● Do daily pelvic floor exercises to improve muscle tone and help prevent leakage – your specialist can help guide you in this.

● Enjoy regular physical activity to stay strong, move well and lose any excess body weight.

● Eat a balanced diet of fruit, vegetables and grains, plus plenty of water to prevent constipation.

For more information, visit the Continence Foundation of Australia; continence.org.au

Reframing menopause in a positive light

THE FACTS

A natural, transitional phase of every woman's life, menopause usually occurs between the ages of 45 and 55, and refers to the date of a woman's final menstrual period. Yet due to the hormonal changes and symptoms that can occur in the lead-up to menopause (known as perimenopause), it's something that many women dread and feel uncomfortable talking about. Consider these steps to embrace menopause as the empowering milestone that it is.

HAVE OPEN CONVERSATIONS

Normalise your experience by starting discussions among your friends and family (male and female), particularly regarding any hormonal changes and symptoms you're experiencing. Embrace the solidarity that comes with hearing about other women's experiences, too.

BE A CHAMPION FOR CHANGE

Not all workplaces are knowledgeable or sympathetic to the challenges that come with menopause. Speak to your employer about your situation and any symptoms that make work difficult, and make reasonable requests for support, such as flexible working hours, uniform alterations to cooler fabrics or the supply of a desktop fan. If comfortable doing so, offer to help develop policies that support menopause at work for all women in your workplace.

LOOK ON THE BRIGHT SIDE

Once you've been through menopause, you can look forward to a host of benefits, with studies finding some post-menopausal women have fewer headaches and mood swings, are less susceptible to hay fever and enjoy greater sexual liberation.

SEE THIS AS A PIVOTAL MOMENT FOR YOUR HEALTH

The average woman will live to 85, so use this new stage of life as an opportunity to implement some healthy lifestyle changes, such as reducing your alcohol intake, quitting smoking, increasing your calcium intake for bone health, finding time for self-care or introducing more activity into your daily routine.

Simple ways to eat more iron

Iron is an important element for our bodies, helping to produce red blood cells, which are essential for a healthy immune system, muscle strength, energy and mental function. If we don't have enough iron, or use more than we consume, we become iron deficient. When you're low in iron, you may experience fatigue, leg cramps, brain fog, insomnia, shortness of breath or lightheadedness. Women are more likely than men to be iron deficient, with up to 18 per cent of otherwise healthy women low in iron. Heavy periods, pregnancy and breastfeeding are the main reasons for this.

If you're experiencing any symptoms of iron deficiency or are worried your iron levels are low, see your GP for a blood test. They may recommend an iron supplement, and there are also lots of dietary ways to increase your iron intake.

RECOMMENDED DAILY INTAKE FOR IRON	
Girls aged 14-18	15mg
Women aged 19-50	18mg
Pregnant women	27mg
Breastfeeding women*	9mg
Women aged 51 and over	8mg

Based on the assumption that menstruation does not resume until after six months of exclusive breastfeeding

FOODS HIGH IN IRON	IRON (MG)
Animal-based options	
Kangaroo (100g)	4.4
Sardines (120g)	3.24
Lean beef (100g)	3.1
Lean lamb (100g)	2.7
Lean pork (100g)	1.4
Egg (55g)	1.1
Plant-based options	
Chickpeas (100g)	6.2
Tofu (100g)	5.2
Iron-fortified cereal (30g)	3
Cashews (50g)	2.5
Baked beans (140g)	2.24
Cooked spinach (1/2 cup)	2.2

BOOST YOUR IRON ABSORPTION
- Start with an iron-rich breakfast to give you energy for the day ahead. Try iron-fortified cereal, eggs or baked beans on wholemeal toast.
- Pair your plant-based iron sources with foods rich in vitamin C, such as oranges, tomatoes and strawberries.
- Calcium can inhibit iron absorption, so avoid combining high-calcium foods, like dairy or calcium-fortified dairy alternatives, in the same meal.

MARCH						
S	M	T	W	T	F	S
30	31					1
2	3	4	5	6	7	8
9	10	11	12	13	14	15
16	17	18	19	20	21	22
23	24	25	26	27	28	29

APRIL						
S	M	T	W	T	F	S
		1	2	3	4	5
6	7	8	9	10	11	12
13	14	15	16	17	18	19
20	21	22	23	24	25	26
27	28	29	30			

MAY						
S	M	T	W	T	F	S
				1	2	3
4	5	6	7	8	9	10
11	12	13	14	15	16	17
18	19	20	21	22	23	24
25	26	27	28	29	30	31

31 MONDAY EID AL-FITR (ISLAMIC HOLIDAY)

1 TUESDAY

2 WEDNESDAY

3 THURSDAY

April
2025

4 FRIDAY

> **MANAGE NIGHT SWEATS DURING MENOPAUSE** by wearing lightweight pyjamas to stay cool, bringing an ice pack to bed and keeping a glass of water nearby.

5 SATURDAY

6 SUNDAY DAYLIGHT SAVING TIME ENDS (ACT, NSW, SA, TAS, VIC)

		MARCH								APRIL								MAY				
S	M	T	W	T	F	S		S	M	T	W	T	F	S		S	M	T	W	T	F	S
30	31					1				1	2	3	4	5						1	2	3
2	3	4	5	6	7	8		6	7	8	9	10	11	12		4	5	6	7	8	9	10
9	10	11	12	13	14	15		13	14	15	16	17	18	19		11	12	13	14	15	16	17
16	17	18	19	20	21	22		20	21	22	23	24	25	26		18	19	20	21	22	23	24
23	24	25	26	27	28	29		27	28	29	30					25	26	27	28	29	30	31

7 MONDAY

8 TUESDAY

9 WEDNESDAY

10 THURSDAY

April 2025

11 FRIDAY

12 SATURDAY

MOTHER'S DAY IS NEXT MONTH. Help save the lives of mums everywhere by making a donation to breast cancer research in lieu of a gift. Visit breastcancertrials. org.au.

13 SUNDAY PALM SUNDAY, PASSOVER BEGINS

MARCH						
S	M	T	W	T	F	S
30	31					1
2	3	4	5	6	7	8
9	10	11	12	13	14	15
16	17	18	19	20	21	22
23	24	25	26	27	28	29

APRIL						
S	M	T	W	T	F	S
		1	2	3	4	5
6	7	8	9	10	11	12
13	14	15	16	17	18	19
20	21	22	23	24	25	26
27	28	29	30			

MAY						
S	M	T	W	T	F	S
				1	2	3
4	5	6	7	8	9	10
11	12	13	14	15	16	17
18	19	20	21	22	23	24
25	26	27	28	29	30	31

14 MONDAY

15 TUESDAY

16 WEDNESDAY

17 THURSDAY

April
2025

18 FRIDAY GOOD FRIDAY

19 SATURDAY

> **FIND A GOOD GP WHO WILL LISTEN** to your concerns and who you feel comfortable with. Don't be afraid to try a few doctors until you find the right one.

20 SUNDAY EASTER SUNDAY

M A R C H						
S	M	T	W	T	F	S
30	31					1
2	3	4	5	6	7	8
9	10	11	12	13	14	15
16	17	18	19	20	21	22
23	24	25	26	27	28	29

A P R I L						
S	M	T	W	T	F	S
		1	2	3	4	5
6	7	8	9	10	11	12
13	14	15	16	17	18	19
20	21	22	23	24	25	26
27	28	29	30			

M A Y						
S	M	T	W	T	F	S
				1	2	3
4	5	6	7	8	9	10
11	12	13	14	15	16	17
18	19	20	21	22	23	24
25	26	27	28	29	30	31

21 MONDAY EASTER MONDAY

22 TUESDAY EASTER TUESDAY (TAS)

23 WEDNESDAY

24 THURSDAY

April
2025

25 FRIDAY <small>ANZAC DAY</small>

26 SATURDAY

27 SUNDAY

"

I was first diagnosed in 2013 which then progressed to metastatic breast cancer in 2018. I felt I had two options: just give up, or be positive and take one day at a time. I'm participating in a clinical trial and hoping this treatment will work so I am around when my granddaughters grow up. I feel safe knowing I'm in good care.

Maria Bodnar,
first diagnosed age 60

let's talk about
HEART HEALTH

Every day, 10 Australian women die from a heart attack and 22 women die of heart disease, with Indigenous women twice as likely to be affected. Read on for the important steps you can take to reduce your heart risk.

It can be a shock to learn that you have a heart condition, and you will no doubt have many questions about how it might affect your health and life moving forward. The good news is that some heart conditions can be managed if found early, so you can continue to enjoy life to its fullest. Familiarise yourself with four common conditions that affect women's heart health and how they're treated.

CONDITION	DESCRIPTION	MANAGEMENT
ARRHYTHMIA	A type of heart condition where the heart rhythm is abnormal. A normal resting heart rate is between 60 and 100 beats per minute. With arrhythmia, the heart may skip a beat, beat irregularly, flutter or race, or beat faster or slower than the normal rate.	Treatment varies based on age and other medical factors, but may involve medication, a procedure or surgery or the implantation of a pacemaker.
HIGH BLOOD PRESSURE (also known as hypertension)	Occurs when blood pressure is higher than normal (140/90mmHg or higher) over a 24-hour period, forcing the heart to work harder to circulate blood around the body. Over time, this can damage the artery walls and other organs, making it a major risk for heart disease.	Blood pressure can be lowered with improved diet and exercise, by quitting smoking and limiting alcohol, and with medication.
HIGH CHOLESTEROL	A fat-like substance that is essential for good health, but can cause harm in excess. There are two types: HDL (good) and LDL (bad). Too much LDL can build up in the arteries, restricting blood flow and increasing the risk of heart disease.	A healthy diet and lifestyle can reduce your bad cholesterol levels, and your doctor may also prescribe medication.
PRE-ECLAMPSIA	A condition where blood pressure increases, usually during the second half of pregnancy. If left untreated, it can pose serious risk to both mother and baby. It usually resolves after birth, but can increase the risk of the mother developing cardiovascular disease later in life.	Depending on your age and the severity, your doctor may recommend going to hospital for monitoring or inducing labour early.

For more information, visit the Victor Chang Cardiac Research Institute; victorchang.edu.au

Heart disease: know your risks

There are a number of risk factors that can increase a woman's likelihood of developing heart disease. Some are linked to lifestyle choices, others are associated with health conditions, and there are risk factors beyond our control. Leading a healthy lifestyle can help reduce our risk, as can having regular heart health check-ups.

The main risk factors for heart disease
Our heart disease risk increases once we turn 45, or 30 for Aboriginal and Torres Strait Islander people. In addition, having diabetes or a family history of heart disease may increase the risk, as can menopause and pregnancy complications like preeclampsia and gestational diabetes. While you can't modify these risks, it's important to flag them with your GP so they can monitor your heart health over time.

The other risk factors, which you can control, include:
- Smoking or vaping
- Poor diet
- Insufficient physical activity
- Alcohol consumption
- High blood pressure and high cholesterol
- Diabetes
- Obesity/being overweight
- Stress and depression
- Poor sleep.

BE PROACTIVE BY TAKING THESE STEPS
- Eat a variety of fresh fruit, vegetables, lean protein and wholegrains, choose unsaturated fats rather than saturated fats and limit salt and refined sugars.
- Be active most (if not all) days, aiming for at least 150-300 minutes of moderate-intensity aerobic activity or at least 75-150 minutes of vigorous activity (or a combination of both) every week.
- Book in for a heart health check with your GP to test your blood pressure, cholesterol and blood sugar levels.
- Take care of your mental health by looking for ways to limit stress triggers in your life and seeking support for anxiety and depression.
- Get seven to nine hours of sleep each night and seek help if you suffer from any chronic sleep disorders.
- Limit alcohol intake to no more than half to one standard drink per day.
- Quit smoking or vaping by calling 13 QUIT (137 848) or visiting quit.org.au.

Warning signs of a heart attack

Along with the well-known heart attack symptoms like chest pain, women can experience different symptoms to men, many of which are subtle and can be easily explained away. Symptoms can vary from person to person, so if you or someone you know experiences one or a combination of the following symptoms, call Triple Zero (000) immediately.

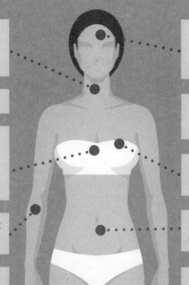

Unusual pain or discomfort in the neck, jaw or shoulder/s

Feeling dizzy, faint, anxious or generally unwell

Breathlessness

Upper back pain or pressure

Chest pain that feels like burning, throbbing, tightness or trapped wind

A racing heart or "fluttering"

Tightness or discomfort in one or both arms

Indigestion, heartburn, nausea or stomach pain

Sweating

Sudden fatigue

Warning signs of a stroke

How do you know if someone is having a stroke? Remember the acronym **FAST.**

FACE. Are their face, eyes or mouth drooping on one or both sides?
ARMS. Can they lift both arms?
SPEECH. Is their speech slurred or garbled? Can they understand you?
TIME TO ACT. If you see any of these signs, call Triple Zero (000) straightaway.

In addition to the above, be aware of these other common symptoms:

- Paralysis, weakness or numbness in the face, arm or leg on one or both sides of the body
- Dizziness, loss of balance or an unexplained fall
- Loss of vision, sudden blurring or decreased vision in one or both eyes
- Severe, abrupt or unexplained headache
- Difficulty swallowing.

7 ways to eat for heart health

Poor diet is one of the leading risk factors for heart disease and can also play a part in causing high blood pressure and high cholesterol, diabetes and weight gain. By making better dietary choices, we can reverse this risk significantly. Here's how.

Eat a rainbow of fresh fruit and vegetables to tick off a range of vitamins and phytonutrients for maximum health benefits. Buy seasonally for extra freshness and don't forget frozen and canned options at other times of the year (check the salt and sugar content).

Limit ultra-processed foods, such as protein bars, packaged snacks, confectionary, biscuits, cakes and fast food, which can raise the risk of heart disease, heart attack and stroke. Where possible, fresh wholefoods and homemade meals are best.

Choose lean protein options, limiting red meat consumption to no more than three times a week. Instead, look to lean poultry, such as skinless chicken breasts and turkey mince, fish, eggs and plant-based protein sources like legumes, tofu, nuts and seeds.

Ease up on the salt. We only need one to two grams of salt a day, as too much can lead to high blood pressure, heart disease and stroke. Check the salt content in packaged foods, and when cooking at home, season food with herbs, spices, chilli or a squeeze of lemon.

Incorporate fibre-rich wholegrains into meals for a healthy digestive system and to assist with cholesterol, blood pressure and weight loss. Get fibre from fruit and vegetables (including the skins), wholegrains and cereals, nuts and seeds.

Cut back on sugar, which can cause weight gain and lead to high blood pressure. Limit sugary treats in favour of fruit or nuts, wean yourself off sugar in your tea or coffee, and swap soft drinks for water and sugary cereals for plain wholegrain options.

Opt for healthy fats and oils, including avocado, olive oil and most nuts and seeds. Avoid saturated fats found in fatty meat, coconut and palm oils as well as trans fats, which are found in fried foods, snack foods and commercially baked goods.

Make every moment brighter

Interflora is synonymous the world over with the feelings and sentiments that only flowers can evoke.

We make a good moment great, bad ones a little lighter and everyday moments a reason to be thankful. From expressions of love, to celebrations of success; from shared sorrows, to saying "I'm sorry".

For more than 70 years we have always been trusted to play a unique part in the lives of our customers. If it's important to you, it's important to us.

Our commitment to excellence in every aspect of our business – from the beauty of a handcrafted floral arrangement to the delivery to your door – has only strengthened during our long and proud history in Australia. And we'll continue to do so, well into the future.

We don't just deliver flowers, but a feeling, a moment and an emotion. Because the act of giving and receiving flowers makes every moment brighter. Always.

#AlwaysInterflora

 InterfloraAU   Interflora_AU    InterfloraAustralia   InterfloraAustralia

		APRIL				
S	M	T	W	T	F	S
		1	2	3	4	5
6	7	8	9	10	11	12
13	14	15	16	17	18	19
20	21	22	23	24	25	26
27	28	29	30			

		MAY				
S	M	T	W	T	F	S
				1	2	3
4	5	6	7	8	9	10
11	12	13	14	15	16	17
18	19	20	21	22	23	24
25	26	27	28	29	30	31

		JUNE				
S	M	T	W	T	F	S
1	2	3	4	5	6	7
8	9	10	11	12	13	14
15	16	17	18	19	20	21
22	23	24	25	26	27	28
29	30					

28 MONDAY

29 TUESDAY

30 WEDNESDAY

1 THURSDAY

May
2025

2 FRIDAY

3 SATURDAY

4 SUNDAY

APRIL						
S	M	T	W	T	F	S
		1	2	3	4	5
6	7	8	9	10	11	12
13	14	15	16	17	18	19
20	21	22	23	24	25	26
27	28	29	30			

MAY						
S	M	T	W	T	F	S
				1	2	3
4	5	6	7	8	9	10
11	12	13	14	15	16	17
18	19	20	21	22	23	24
25	26	27	28	29	30	31

JUNE						
S	M	T	W	T	F	S
1	2	3	4	5	6	7
8	9	10	11	12	13	14
15	16	17	18	19	20	21
22	23	24	25	26	27	28
29	30					

5 MONDAY LABOUR DAY (QLD), MAY DAY (NT)

6 TUESDAY

7 WEDNESDAY

8 THURSDAY

May 2025

9 FRIDAY

10 SATURDAY

11 SUNDAY MOTHER'S DAY

APRIL
S	M	T	W	T	F	S
		1	2	3	4	5
6	7	8	9	10	11	12
13	14	15	16	17	18	19
20	21	22	23	24	25	26
27	28	29	30			

MAY
S	M	T	W	T	F	S
				1	2	3
4	5	6	7	8	9	10
11	12	13	14	15	16	17
18	19	20	21	22	23	24
25	26	27	28	29	30	31

JUNE
S	M	T	W	T	F	S
1	2	3	4	5	6	7
8	9	10	11	12	13	14
15	16	17	18	19	20	21
22	23	24	25	26	27	28
29	30					

12 MONDAY

13 TUESDAY

14 WEDNESDAY

15 THURSDAY

May
2025

16 FRIDAY

17 SATURDAY

ANYONE AGED 45 AND OVER, or 30 for Indigenous people, is entitled to a free Heart Health Check. Download the Heart Health Check Guide from victorchang.edu.au to track your results.

18 SUNDAY

APRIL						
S	M	T	W	T	F	S
		1	2	3	4	5
6	7	8	9	10	11	12
13	14	15	16	17	18	19
20	21	22	23	24	25	26
27	28	29	30			

MAY						
S	M	T	W	T	F	S
				1	2	3
4	5	6	7	8	9	10
11	12	13	14	15	16	17
18	19	20	21	22	23	24
25	26	27	28	29	30	31

JUNE						
S	M	T	W	T	F	S
1	2	3	4	5	6	7
8	9	10	11	12	13	14
15	16	17	18	19	20	21
22	23	24	25	26	27	28
29	30					

19 MONDAY

20 TUESDAY

21 WEDNESDAY

22 THURSDAY

23 FRIDAY

24 SATURDAY

DID YOU KNOW EXCESSIVE NOISE AND LIGHT can affect your heart? Try noise-cancelling earphones in noisy environments and choose warm (yellow) lighting rather than cool (white/blue).

25 SUNDAY

		APRIL								MAY								JUNE				
S	M	T	W	T	F	S		S	M	T	W	T	F	S		S	M	T	W	T	F	S
		1	2	3	4	5						1	2	3		1	2	3	4	5	6	7
6	7	8	9	10	11	12		4	5	6	7	8	9	10		8	9	10	11	12	13	14
13	14	15	16	17	18	19		11	12	13	14	15	16	17		15	16	17	18	19	20	21
20	21	22	23	24	25	26		18	19	20	21	22	23	24		22	23	24	25	26	27	28
27	28	29	30					25	26	27	28	29	30	31		29	30					

26 MONDAY   NATIONAL SORRY DAY

27 TUESDAY

28 WEDNESDAY

29 THURSDAY

30 FRIDAY

31 SATURDAY

MAKE SMALL CHANGES for heart health. Choose vegie-loaded takeaway options, try a new form of exercise or sign up for Dry July to reduce your alcohol intake.

1 SUNDAY

66

I had breast pain and tests showed I had breast cancer, which had spread to my bones and spine. I feel lucky to be participating in a clinical trial and I'm getting stronger day by day. Because of clinical trials, there are other treatment options for me if this doesn't work. I hope to get better and be happ

Sham Lachin, first diagnosed age 39

let's talk about
YOUR FINANCES

Statistically, women are at a financial disadvantage to men. But you can change the narrative and take charge of your fiscal future by gaining a better understanding of your spending habits and needs.

Every day we make choices about our money by saving, spending or investing in our future. Each of these decisions, big or small, can have an impact on our financial wellbeing, and ultimately, our lifestyle and mental health. For women, financial wellbeing can be more challenging to achieve, due to gender pay gaps, taking time off work to care for children and a lack of financial knowledge. Follow these steps to improve your financial wellbeing.

MANAGE YOUR EVERYDAY EXPENSES
To understand your spending patterns, make a list of all essential expenses, such as rent, mortgage repayments, phone, internet, electricity, water and gas, and how often you pay them. Also track your variable expenses, including petrol, groceries, medical treatments, personal purchases, gifts and entertainment, over a month.

PLAN FOR EMERGENCIES
Having money set aside for unexpected expenses – for example, car repairs, medical emergencies or last-minute travel – will give you peace of mind and improve your ability to cope with financial stress. Aim to put aside money each week to build up a rainy-day fund over time.

PREPARE FOR YOUR FUTURE
Set some financial goals – an overseas trip, saving for a new home or a comfortable retirement – and a plan of how you'll achieve them. Think about how much money you'll need to achieve each goal and when you want to achieve it by. Now calculate how much you need to save each week or month to get there.

BALANCE YOUR BUDGET
A successful budget covers the above three areas of financial wellbeing – everyday spending, savings and future spending. Looking at all three categories side by side can help identify ways to reduce spending in one area to cater for another. If you're spending more than you earn, or don't earn enough to cover all three eventualities, take action by cutting out non-essential expenses or looking for better deals.

USE THE 'BUCKET' SYSTEM
One way to stick to your plan is to set up different bank accounts for essentials, spending, savings and future savings and transfer funds into them every month. This means you're not spending money that is earmarked for savings and vice versa. Look for accounts with low or no fees, or high interest rates if they're for savings.

Simple solutions to bad spending habits

A couple of dollars spent here or there may not seem like a big deal, but over time, those small costs and purchases can add up and eat away at your savings. Here are six common spending pitfalls, that if eliminated, could see your bank balance grow.

4 Paying for unused subscriptions Do you subscribe to streaming services, gym memberships, loyalty programs, software or apps that you don't often use? Go through your credit card statement to identify any services that can be cancelled or put on hold.

5 Staying with the same provider Don't be complacent. Compare your mortgage, electricity, superannuation, mobile phone, internet and insurance rates against other providers, and don't be afraid to take your business elsewhere to benefit from discounts and extra savings.

1 Online shopping traps This might include adding extra items to your cart to qualify for free shipping, impulse buying or failing to return unsuitable items. Plan your purchases carefully, ordering what you need from the same store(s) if possible. And dedicate time each week or month to check invoices and process returns.

2 Grocery shopping without a list Wandering aimlessly up and down the aisles will put you at risk of making impulse purchases or buying surplus items. Try to write a list based on the week's meal plan and limit supermarket visits to once a week.

3 Buying bottled water Why pay for water when we have access to clean, drinkable tap water? Make a habit of taking a reusable bottle with you when you go out or have a few so you can leave one in the car, one at work, one in your bag.

6 Too much takeaway A barista coffee in the morning, lunch at a cafe in between appointments, takeaway when you don't want to cook... it all adds up. Set yourself a takeaway or eating out budget for the month and meal plan at home to make sure you don't deviate from it.

FIND WAYS TO EARN ADDITIONAL INCOME, such as selling items you no longer need, looking for casual work or signing up to be a meal delivery driver.

Dealing with financial stress

Recent inflation and interest rate rises are putting an increasing amount of stress on household budgets, with older Australians, single parents, small business owners, students, those on low or unstable incomes and women more susceptible to financial stress. Financial stress can have a detrimental effect on our mental health, and can also impact our self-esteem, relationships, work productivity and quality of life. Use these practical tips to regain financial stability.

SHORT-TERM SOLUTIONS

- Contact the National Debt Helpline (1800 007 007) or Mob Strong Debt Help for Aboriginal and Torres Strait Islander people (1800 808 488) and ask to speak with a financial counsellor for free.

- Get in touch with the organisations you owe money to and negotiate an extension or new payment terms based on what you can afford.

- Contact local charities and organisations who can provide assistance in the form of groceries, vouchers and housing.

- Consider a no-interest loan for people on low incomes or victims of family and domestic violence.

- Look into whether you qualify for Government financial supports, such as JobSeeker, family assistance, youth allowance or Crisis Payment.

CHANGES TO MAKE FOR THE LONG-TERM

- Create a budget to resolve current financial problems and avoid more in the future. Use the budget planner at the front of this diary.

- Prioritise debt repayment, starting with the debts with the highest interest charges. Even better, consolidate into one low-interest loan.

- Keep a journal to identify spending triggers (shopping when you're stressed, overspending to assist others) and possible solutions.

- Create a worry time. Don't let your financial stress be all-consuming. Have a designated time to look at bills and balances, make calls and come up with strategies.

- Make time for things you enjoy. Happy moments will help alleviate stress and give you perspective. It doesn't need to be costly – go for a walk, swim at the beach, visit friends or join a community group.

The bank of Mum and Dad – pros & cons

According to research, up to 60 per cent of first-home buyers are receiving financial help from their parents, and many parents are assisting their adult children in other ways, by lending them money to cover bills, helping with childcare or allowing children to stay at home or move back home while they study or save towards their future. This sort of financial assistance can come with advantages and disadvantages. Take a look to see if it's right for your family situation.

THE PROS

- Getting financial assistance from Mum and Dad can make large purchases, like a home or car, more attainable sooner.
- Loans from family members often come with low or no interest rates and flexible repayment terms.
- If receiving their parents' help with a home deposit, home buyers may avoid paying mortgage insurance, which is typically required by lenders when the deposit is less than 20 per cent of the property value.
- Adult children living at home can be great company as parents get older. Household responsibilities and bills can be shared.
- Parents can help their children now, rather than leaving them money in their wills.

THE CONS

- Not all parents can afford to help their children financially.
- All loans should be put in writing, and both parties should seek independent legal advice.
- Loans between family members can potentially create tension if repayment terms are not met, or resentment among siblings if all don't benefit equally.
- Lending a substantial amount to children or allowing them to live in the family home for longer may then have a negative impact on the parents' financial security, ability to downsize and plans for retirement.
- Adult children might not learn financial independence and responsibility if they rely on assistance from Mum and Dad.

BREAST CANCER TRIALS

Will you join us?

The researchers at Breast Cancer Trials are inspired by the growing community of supporters nationwide who raise funds to make life-saving research possible.

By hosting a fundraiser, participating in a walking challenge, or entering a fitness event, there's many ways you can join our 'no more lives cut short' movement.

Walk or run 100km's during the month of July and be part of an incredible community who'll cheer you on with every step!

Grab your four-legged friend and participate in our 'pawsome' 57km Dog Walk Challenge over the month of February. Go walkies to save lives!

Are you a keen golfer? Reach out to your local golf club to organise a 'Tee Off' golf event. A perfect reason to get out on the green with your friends.

Host a fundraiser like a morning tea, pamper party or formal dinner – the choice is yours! Get your work colleagues together, or spend time with family and friends.

Put on your joggers and compete in a fitness event. There are many throughout Australia. Register on our website and select Breast Cancer Trials as your charity.

YOU CAN HELP STOP BREAST CANCER THREATENING THE LIVES, HOPES AND DREAMS OF OUR LOVED ONES.

FOR MORE INFORMATION ON THESE EVENTS AND MORE:

Scan this QR code
Visit breastcancertrials.org.au/fundraise

Email fundraising@bctrials.org.au
Phone 1800 423 444

		M A Y								J U N E								J U L Y				
S	M	T	W	T	F	S	S	M	T	W	T	F	S	S	M	T	W	T	F	S
				1	2	3	1	2	3	4	5	6	7			1	2	3	4	5
4	5	6	7	8	9	10	8	9	10	11	12	13	14	6	7	8	9	10	11	12
11	12	13	14	15	16	17	15	16	17	18	19	20	21	13	14	15	16	17	18	19
18	19	20	21	22	23	24	22	23	24	25	26	27	28	20	21	22	23	24	25	26
25	26	27	28	29	30	31	29	30						27	28	29	30	31		

2 MONDAY WESTERN AUSTRALIA DAY (WA), RECONCILIATION DAY (ACT)

3 TUESDAY

4 WEDNESDAY

5 THURSDAY

June 2025

6 FRIDAY QUEENSLAND DAY (QLD)

7 SATURDAY EID AL-ADHA (ISLAMIC HOLIDAY)

IN THE POSITION TO BOOST your superannuation? Use the Super Contributions Optimiser at moneysmart. gov.au to find the best contribution options for you.

8 SUNDAY

			MAY							JUNE							JULY			
S	M	T	W	T	F	S	S	M	T	W	T	F	S	S	M	T	W	T	F	S
				1	2	3	1	2	3	4	5	6	7			1	2	3	4	5
4	5	6	7	8	9	10	8	9	10	11	12	13	14	6	7	8	9	10	11	12
11	12	13	14	15	16	17	15	16	17	18	19	20	21	13	14	15	16	17	18	19
18	19	20	21	22	23	24	22	23	24	25	26	27	28	20	21	22	23	24	25	26
25	26	27	28	29	30	31	29	30						27	28	29	30	31		

9 MONDAY KING'S BIRTHDAY (ACT, NSW, NT, SA, TAS, VIC)

10 TUESDAY

11 WEDNESDAY

12 THURSDAY

June
2025

13 FRIDAY

14 SATURDAY

15 SUNDAY

		MAY				
S	M	T	W	T	F	S
					1	2	3
4	5	6	7	8	9	10
11	12	13	14	15	16	17
18	19	20	21	22	23	24
25	26	27	28	29	30	31

		JUNE				
S	M	T	W	T	F	S
1	2	3	4	5	6	7
8	9	10	11	12	13	14
15	16	17	18	19	20	21
22	23	24	25	26	27	28
29	30					

		JULY				
S	M	T	W	T	F	S
			1	2	3	4	5
6	7	8	9	10	11	12
13	14	15	16	17	18	19
20	21	22	23	24	25	26
27	28	29	30	31		

16 MONDAY

17 TUESDAY

18 WEDNESDAY

19 THURSDAY

June
2025

20 FRIDAY

21 SATURDAY

22 SUNDAY

			MAY			
S	M	T	W	T	F	S
					1	2	3
4	5	6	7	8	9	10
11	12	13	14	15	16	17
18	19	20	21	22	23	24
25	26	27	28	29	30	31

			JUNE			
S	M	T	W	T	F	S
1	2	3	4	5	6	7
8	9	10	11	12	13	14
15	16	17	18	19	20	21
22	23	24	25	26	27	28
29	30					

			JULY			
S	M	T	W	T	F	S
				1	2	3	4	5
6	7	8	9	10	11	12
13	14	15	16	17	18	19
20	21	22	23	24	25	26
27	28	29	30	31		

23 MONDAY

24 TUESDAY

25 WEDNESDAY

26 THURSDAY

June
2025

27 FRIDAY MUHARRAM/ISLAMIC NEW YEAR

28 SATURDAY

IF MONEY IS TIGHT, many banks and utility providers now allow you to pay bills or split large purchases into more manageable instalments.

29 SUNDAY

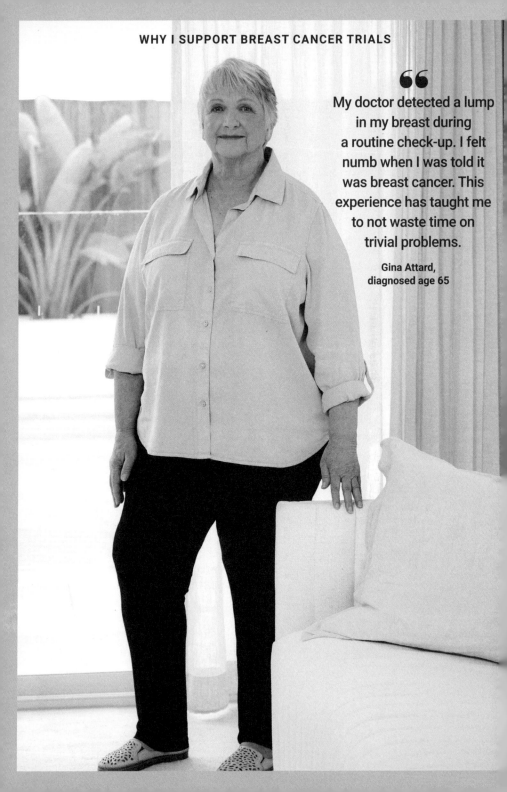

"

My doctor detected a lump in my breast during a routine check-up. I felt numb when I was told it was breast cancer. This experience has taught me to not waste time on trivial problems.

Gina Attard,
diagnosed age 65

let's talk about
AGEING

There is much to be enjoyed in the later stages of life. Put yourself in good stead by staying active, keeping on top of your evolving health needs and shifting your mindset to embrace a new chapter.

Many women experience a sense of dissatisfaction, restlessness and uncertainty when they reach their 40s and 50s. Having spent the first half of their lives studying, working or raising a family, the questions arise: Am I living my best life? And what comes next? The onset of menopause, children moving out of home and coming to terms with their own mortality can add to the feelings of discontent. Reframe this negative mindset with a few simple strategies.

4 WAYS TO EMBRACE MIDDLE AGE

1 **Reflect and reset.** Looking back on your life so far, identify the moments when you were happy and consider how you can cultivate joy in the years ahead. Also acknowledge any low points and how they shaped you. Let go of relationships that didn't serve you well and nurture those that make you happy. You might even consider a sea change or a career change – now is the perfect time for a fresh start.

2 **Choose an active lifestyle.** These mid-years are a great time to take charge of your health and make changes to benefit you in the future. Instead of taking the view that life is all downhill from here, take a proactive stance on your health by making regular exercise part of your future lifestyle. Find activities that you enjoy so it doesn't feel like a chore – even better if you can enjoy them with friends and family.

3 **Shift the focus to you.** In your younger years, you may have prioritised the needs of others – your partner, children, parents, friends or colleagues – over your own. But as you approach this latter half of life, it's time to make more room for you. As children grow up and work priorities shift, take this opportunity to rediscover old interests, pick up a new hobby or start ticking off those bucket-list items.

4 **Seek support.** Mid-life pivots are not always easy to navigate. Talk to friends and family about your future plans and aspirations, or reach out to your GP or a therapist for helpful strategies to navigate this transition.

The signs that you should have your eyes checked

Do you find it difficult to focus on nearby objects or read things that are in front of you? This is a common occurrence faced by most people after the age of 40, as the lens inside the eye becomes less flexible over time. Like the rest of our bodies, our eyes change with time, and as we get older, conditions including cataracts, glaucoma, macular degeneration and diabetic retinopathy can become more commonplace. It's recommended that all Australians aged 65 and over schedule a yearly eye test with an optometrist, or sooner if you notice any of the below signs.

SIGNS YOUR EYESIGHT IS DETERIORATING

Blurred or hazy vision; difficulty seeing details, reading or recognising faces

———

Frequent squinting

———

Visual disturbances – spots, flashes of light, halos or clouds that move across your vision

———

Eye pain, strain or fatigue

———

Reduced colour vision

———

Increased sensitivity to glare

———

Dry eyes

———

Headaches

———

Excessively watery eyes

———

Distorted or double vision

———

Night vision difficulties.

For more information, visit Good vision for life; goodvisionforlife.com.au

Exercise options to increase longevity

As we get older, exercise becomes a useful tool that can help us to not only live longer, but get more out of the years that we have left. Regular exercise comes with a host of benefits including preserving muscle mass and strength, maintaining heart health, assisting with cognitive (brain) function, enhancing bone density, improving balance and reducing the effects of stress, anxiety and depression – all of which are important factors as we age.

For a well-rounded routine, Australians aged 65 and over should aim for at least 30 minutes of moderate-intensity activity on most if not all days. This should include activities that increase heart rate as well as strength, flexibility and balance.

If you have a health condition, speak with your doctor to find the right activity for you. Even a small increase in activity can do wonders for your health and wellbeing and improve your quality of life going forward.

TRY THESE OPTIONS TO COVER ALL OF YOUR NEEDS	Muscles	Weight	Bones	Heart	Balance	Mood	Mind	Flexibility
BRISK WALKING	✔	✔	✔	✔	✔	✔	✔	✔
GARDENING	✔	✔	✔	✔	✔	✔	✔	✔
RESISTANCE TRAINING	✔	✔	✔	✔	✔	✔	✔	✔
TAI CHI	✔	✔	✔	✔	✔	✔	✔	✔
DANCING	✔	✔	✔	✔	✔	✔	✔	✔
YOGA	✔	✔	✔	✔	✔	✔	✔	✔

Living with chronic pain

More than 3.6 million Australians currently live with chronic pain, including one in five people over the age of 45 and one in four people over 85. Defined as persistent pain that lasts for more than three months, it can be caused by illness, musculoskeletal problems, injury, surgery or cancer, and in some cases, the cause is unknown.

Chronic pain is often referred to as an invisible illness, where you can feel pain 24/7 without appearing unwell to those around you. This can take a huge toll on a person's mood and emotional wellbeing, and living with this constant pain can make it difficult to work, care for yourself and do the things you enjoy.

To manage the effects of chronic pain, a multidisciplinary approach is usually recommended, using a combination of treatment strategies including medication, movement, diet, relaxation, mindfulness and psychology. You may need to see a team of health professionals to meet all of these needs, including your GP, a pain specialist, physiotherapist, psychologist, occupational therapist or dietitian.

For more information, visit Chronic Pain Australia; chronicpainaustralia.org.au

9 brain-boosting foods

It's natural for our brains to change with age. Fat deposits inside the brain cells (neurons) can limit brain function and old brain cells may die and not grow back. Some prescription medications can affect our cognitive abilities while certain diseases, such as Alzheimer's disease, become more prevalent with old age. But that doesn't mean you'll automatically become forgetful or lose mental clarity, and a healthy diet may be able to help boost brain function and stave off these markers of decline. Fill your plate with these healthy options.

WHOLEGRAINS Brown rice, quinoa and oats are high in fibre and B-group vitamins for mental wellbeing, and release slowly into the body for sustained brain fuel.

PLANT-BASED OILS Olive oil, peanut oil and coconut oil are rich in polyphenols, which are thought to help reverse cognitive deficits brought on by ageing.

NUTS AND SEEDS Walnuts, almonds, chia seeds and pumpkin seeds contain vitamin E, omega-3 fats and manganese to nurture and protect brain cells.

FATTY FISH Omega-3 fatty acids in salmon, tuna and sardines have the potential to improve memory and protect brain cells when consumed regularly.

BERRIES The antioxidants, flavonoids and anthocyanins in deep-coloured berries like blueberries, blackberries and mulberries may help reduce rates of cognitive decline.

FERMENTED FOODS Stock up on kimchi, kombucha, miso, yoghurt and pickled vegetables for their probiotics, which support memory and cognition.

LEAFY GREENS Rich in antioxidants, green vegies grown above ground (kale, broccoli, spinach) can assist in building brain pathways to slow cognitive decline.

AVOCADO It's high in zinc, omega-3 fats, potassium and monounsaturated fats to improve mood, combat fatigue and reduce the risk of Alzheimer's disease.

EGGS They deliver a healthy dose of choline (which is converted into acetylcholine to aid memory function) and cholesterol (to protect our brain cells).

		J U N E				
S	M	T	W	T	F	S
1	2	3	4	5	6	7
8	9	10	11	12	13	14
15	16	17	18	19	20	21
22	23	24	25	26	27	28
29	30					

		J U L Y				
S	M	T	W	T	F	S
		1	2	3	4	5
6	7	8	9	10	11	12
13	14	15	16	17	18	19
20	21	22	23	24	25	26
27	28	29	30	31		

		A U G U S T				
S	M	T	W	T	F	S
31					1	2
3	4	5	6	7	8	9
10	11	12	13	14	15	16
17	18	19	20	21	22	23
24	25	26	27	28	29	30

30 MONDAY

1 TUESDAY

2 WEDNESDAY

3 THURSDAY

July
2025

4 FRIDAY

5 SATURDAY

RESIST REACHING FOR THE WINE at the end of a stressful day, and instead go for a walk, call a friend for a chat or sing along to your favourite song.

6 SUNDAY NAIDOC WEEK BEGINS

J U N E						
S	M	T	W	T	F	S
1	2	3	4	5	6	7
8	9	10	11	12	13	14
15	16	17	18	19	20	21
22	23	24	25	26	27	28
29	30					

J U L Y						
S	M	T	W	T	F	S
		1	2	3	4	5
6	7	8	9	10	11	12
13	14	15	16	17	18	19
20	21	22	23	24	25	26
27	28	29	30	31		

A U G U S T						
S	M	T	W	T	F	S
31					1	2
3	4	5	6	7	8	9
10	11	12	13	14	15	16
17	18	19	20	21	22	23
24	25	26	27	28	29	30

7 MONDAY

8 TUESDAY

9 WEDNESDAY

10 THURSDAY

July
2025

11 FRIDAY

12 SATURDAY

CHECK YOUR HOME FOR TRIP HAZARDS including loose carpets, broken tiles, inadequate lighting, cluttered walkways or trailing power cords.

13 SUNDAY

		J U N E							J U L Y							A U G U S T			
S	M	T	W	T	F	S	S	M	T	W	T	F	S	S	M	T	W	T	F	S
1	2	3	4	5	6	7			1	2	3	4	5	31					1	2
8	9	10	11	12	13	14	6	7	8	9	10	11	12	3	4	5	6	7	8	9
15	16	17	18	19	20	21	13	14	15	16	17	18	19	10	11	12	13	14	15	16
22	23	24	25	26	27	28	20	21	22	23	24	25	26	17	18	19	20	21	22	23
29	30						27	28	29	30	31			24	25	26	27	28	29	30

14 MONDAY BASTILLE DAY (FRANCE)

15 TUESDAY

16 WEDNESDAY

17 THURSDAY

18 FRIDAY

19 SATURDAY

CHECK IN REGULARLY with elderly neighbours, relatives and friends to reduce feelings of isolation. Use the phone, video calls or group messaging apps if distance is an issue.

20 SUNDAY

		J U N E				
S	M	T	W	T	F	S
1	2	3	4	5	6	7
8	9	10	11	12	13	14
15	16	17	18	19	20	21
22	23	24	25	26	27	28
29	30					

		J U L Y				
S	M	T	W	T	F	S
		1	2	3	4	5
6	7	8	9	10	11	12
13	14	15	16	17	18	19
20	21	22	23	24	25	26
27	28	29	30	31		

		A U G U S T				
S	M	T	W	T	F	S
31					1	2
3	4	5	6	7	8	9
10	11	12	13	14	15	16
17	18	19	20	21	22	23
24	25	26	27	28	29	30

21 MONDAY

22 TUESDAY

23 WEDNESDAY

24 THURSDAY

July
2025

25 FRIDAY

26 SATURDAY

> **PREVENT COMPUTER-INDUCED EYE STRAIN** by taking regular breaks away from your screen and positioning devices at least an arm's length from your face.

27 SUNDAY

"

My daughter was just two weeks old when I was diagnosed. I was overwhelmed – I had three kids and a husband who needed me. Once I understood the treatment plan, things became less daunting. Having this photo taken the day after I marked seven years cancer free is very special.

Jodie-Anne Brown, diagnosed age 35, pictured with her family

let's talk about
FAMILY

Caring for a family can present numerous challenges, from catering for a range of nutritional needs to fighting illness and establishing good habits. Strike the right balance with these tips.

I t's never too early to teach young children healthy habits. Not only will it help support their growth and development, statistics show they'll be more likely to carry these healthy habits into adulthood. Role modelling is also important – set a good example and your kids will take their cues from you. Start by instilling these five healthy habits as early as possible.

1 Healthy eating
Make healthy eating the norm by serving children a variety of nutritious foods, and limiting heavily processed and sugary foods. Where possible, enjoy meals together as a family, and depending on your child's age, get them involved with planning, shopping and preparing meals.

2 Staying active
Make physical activity a part of your family's routine by going for regular walks, bike rides or swims together. Encourage children to try group activities, too, which can help boost their self-esteem and extend their friendship circles.

3 Personal hygiene
Good hygiene is important for cleanliness and helps prevent the spread of germs. Teach children to do the following: wash their hands when dirty, after using the toilet, before eating and after touching animals; cover their mouth when they sneeze, or cough into their elbow; have regular baths and showers; brush and floss their teeth twice a day (you can help with this until the age of seven or eight).

4 Balanced screen time
With screens (TVs, computers, tablets and phones) a constant presence in our lives, it's important to have clear rules and discussions around screen time, and to provide opportunities for family time, creative play and physical activity to help children strike the right balance. The Australian government recommends children aged two to five have no more than one hour of screen time per day and kids aged 5 to 17 have no more than two hours per day (not including schoolwork).

5 Sun safety
From three years of age, children should be encouraged to apply their own sunscreen with supervision. Set up a sunscreen station in front of a mirror or make up a song or poster to help them remember where to apply it.

For more information, visit Triple P – Positive Parenting Program; triplep-parenting.net.au

Simple lunchbox tips for the whole family

Forget the Instagram-worthy, bento-style lunchbox – when it comes to making your child's (and your own) lunch, simple is best. Keep these tips in mind to take the stress out of this daily task.

- Children often don't have much time to eat, and will be keen to play. Stick with things they can eat with their hands, like sandwiches, fruit, cut-up vegetables, crackers or cheese.
- Make it budget-friendly by buying fruit and vegetables in season and serving the same snacks throughout the week to avoid wastage.
- Don't overthink it. Look at the foods your child enjoys at home and send a portable version of that to school. Insulated flasks are great for keeping dinner leftovers hot for lunch.
- While variety has its benefits, don't be afraid to send a similar lunch every day, and introduce more variety at breakfast or dinner time. The same applies to work lunches – make a week's worth of salads, soups or wraps at the start of the week to save time and money.
- Get older children involved. Plan what you'll make, go grocery shopping together and prepare lunchboxes the night before so they can watch or help.
- Many teens prefer to buy their lunch from the canteen. Look at the menu together and agree on some nutritious, affordable options. If you can, pre-order online to avoid impulse buys.
- Remember the five core food groups when assembling lunchboxes – use the handy diagram below as a guide.

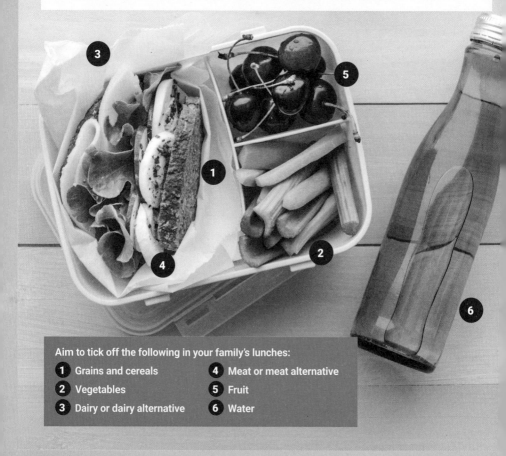

Aim to tick off the following in your family's lunches:

1. Grains and cereals
2. Vegetables
3. Dairy or dairy alternative
4. Meat or meat alternative
5. Fruit
6. Water

Positive ways to parent after a divorce

Of the 49,241 divorces granted in 2022, almost half of these were couples with children. And while there can be many reasons behind a marriage breakdown, most parents will want to help ease the transition for their children and ensure they continue to thrive. Here's how.

TALK OPENLY. Without going into all the details of the break-up, your child deserves to know what is happening and how it will affect them. Listen to their questions and think carefully before answering. Be positive about the future while reassuring them that their worries and feelings are valid, and share your own feelings in a calm, constructive way.

KEEP THINGS CIVIL. When speaking to or about your ex-partner, stay positive and respectful. Don't criticise or belittle them in front of the kids and never make your children take sides or act as a go-between.

DEVELOP A JOINT PARENTING PLAN. Consider what's best for your child when making parenting arrangements – shared custody isn't always the best option. If the child lives with one parent, ensure they see the other parent regularly. Consider attending key events together, like school concerts, graduations or birthday celebrations.

BE CONSISTENT. Routines help children feel secure, safe and in control. Try to continue the routines that matter to your child, working with your ex-partner to maintain the same daily routine of bedtimes and mealtimes, and be consistent with chores, discipline and homework.

MAKE TIME FOR FUN. Spend quality time with the kids to help relieve feelings of sadness or stress. Go for a bush walk, bake together, get manicures or take them to the movies or out to dinner.

6 ways to beat the common cold

By the time we reach adulthood, we have generally built up a good immunity to many cold viruses. However, if you're a parent of young children, aged 60 and over or have a compromised immune system, you might be more susceptible to sickness.

Why do we catch so many colds?
There are more than 200 types of viruses that can cause the common cold (also called an upper respiratory tract infection), all of which are spread by sneezing, coughing and touch. Spending time in close proximity to sick family members, in confined quarters, such as in an office, or in jobs that expose you to germs, such as teaching, can increase your likelihood of getting sick. In winter, lower temperatures reduce our body's ability to fight cold viruses. Poor sleep, dehydration, lack of exercise and ineffective hand washing can also weaken the immune system.

TRY THESE COLD-FIGHTING MEASURES

1 Wash hands frequently with warm, soapy water. Hand washing should last roughly the time it takes to sing the "Happy birthday" song twice. Use hand sanitiser when out and about.

2 Where possible, limit your exposure to people who are sick, or wear a mask in high-risk settings. Postpone social plans when unwell and stay home to avoid spreading illness to others.

3 Keep your immune system functioning properly by enjoying regular physical activity, drinking two litres of water a day and aiming for seven to nine hours of sleep each night.

4 Eat beneficial foods rich in vitamin D (salmon, eggs, fortified milk), zinc (seafood, nuts), flavonoids (blueberries, citrus) and probiotics (kombucha, yoghurt, sauerkraut).

5 Avoid sharing drink bottles, cups, utensils and toothbrushes with family members, and disinfect common items like phones, remotes or keyboards with alcohol wipes.

6 Get vaccinated. While there is no cure for a cold, you can boost your immune system and protect yourself from the flu and COVID-19 by staying up to date with vaccinations.

Self-care strategies for busy parents

Being a parent or a grandparent can take a huge toll on your physical, mental and emotional wellbeing. Juggling the needs of a family while working and running a household might mean that there is little time left for you. To take proper care of ourselves, we need to enjoy regular exercise, eat healthy food, get plenty of rest and prioritise self-care. Doing something for yourself can help relieve stress and boost resilience, patience and positivity, and it doesn't need to cost a lot or take up much time. Here are some self-care ideas to help you get started.

IF YOU HAVE 1 MINUTE...
Drink a glass of water
Hug your partner
Snuggle with your pet
Take some deep breaths
Light a scented candle

IF YOU HAVE 5 MINUTES...
Spend time in the garden
Meditate
Write in your journal
Flick through a magazine or catalogue
Listen to your favourite song

IF YOU HAVE 10 MINUTES...
Paint your nails or put on a face mask
Sit outside with a cup of tea or a book
Do some yoga stretches
Have an uninterrupted shower
Do a crossword, Sudoku or Wordle puzzle

IF YOU HAVE 30 MINUTES...
Run yourself a bath and add soothing bath salts
Take a nap
Go for a walk
Call a friend or loved one
Declutter a room, your handbag or your inbox

IF YOU HAVE 60 MINUTES...
Take up a new hobby or one that has lapsed
Catch up with friends who make you feel good
Listen to an inspiring podcast
Watch an episode of your favourite show
Bake something delicious

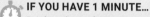

		JULY				
S	M	T	W	T	F	S
		1	2	3	4	5
6	7	8	9	10	11	12
13	14	15	16	17	18	19
20	21	22	23	24	25	26
27	28	29	30	31		

		AUGUST				
S	M	T	W	T	F	S
31					1	2
3	4	5	6	7	8	9
10	11	12	13	14	15	16
17	18	19	20	21	22	23
24	25	26	27	28	29	30

		SEPTEMBER				
S	M	T	W	T	F	S
	1	2	3	4	5	6
7	8	9	10	11	12	13
14	15	16	17	18	19	20
21	22	23	24	25	26	27
28	29	30				

28 MONDAY

29 TUESDAY

30 WEDNESDAY

31 THURSDAY

August 2025

1 FRIDAY

2 SATURDAY

3 SUNDAY

	JULY							AUGUST							SEPTEMBER					
S	M	T	W	T	F	S	S	M	T	W	T	F	S	S	M	T	W	T	F	S
		1	2	3	4	5	31					1	2			1	2	3	4	5	6
6	7	8	9	10	11	12	3	4	5	6	7	8	9	7	8	9	10	11	12	13
13	14	15	16	17	18	19	10	11	12	13	14	15	16	14	15	16	17	18	19	20
20	21	22	23	24	25	26	17	18	19	20	21	22	23	21	22	23	24	25	26	27
27	28	29	30	31			24	25	26	27	28	29	30	28	29	30				

4 MONDAY BANK HOLIDAY (NSW), PICNIC DAY (NT)

5 TUESDAY

6 WEDNESDAY

7 THURSDAY

August
2025

8 FRIDAY

9 SATURDAY

TREAT COLD SYMPTOMS with rest, fluids and paracetamol if needed. Try saline nasal drops for blocked noses or one teaspoon of honey (over 12 months of age) to reduce coughing.

10 SUNDAY

JULY						
S	M	T	W	T	F	S
		1	2	3	4	5
6	7	8	9	10	11	12
13	14	15	16	17	18	19
20	21	22	23	24	25	26
27	28	29	30	31		

AUGUST						
S	M	T	W	T	F	S
31					1	2
3	4	5	6	7	8	9
10	11	12	13	14	15	16
17	18	19	20	21	22	23
24	25	26	27	28	29	30

SEPTEMBER						
S	M	T	W	T	F	S
	1	2	3	4	5	6
7	8	9	10	11	12	13
14	15	16	17	18	19	20
21	22	23	24	25	26	27
28	29	30				

11 MONDAY

12 TUESDAY

13 WEDNESDAY

14 THURSDAY

August
2025

15 FRIDAY

16 SATURDAY

BE FAMILIAR WITH THE APPS AND WEBSITES your child is using and whether they're safe and age-appropriate. Utilise parent controls and security filters where needed.

17 SUNDAY

JULY

S	M	T	W	T	F	S
		1	2	3	4	5
6	7	8	9	10	11	12
13	14	15	16	17	18	19
20	21	22	23	24	25	26
27	28	29	30	31		

AUGUST

S	M	T	W	T	F	S
31					1	2
3	4	5	6	7	8	9
10	11	12	13	14	15	16
17	18	19	20	21	22	23
24	25	26	27	28	29	30

SEPTEMBER

S	M	T	W	T	F	S
	1	2	3	4	5	6
7	8	9	10	11	12	13
14	15	16	17	18	19	20
21	22	23	24	25	26	27
28	29	30				

18 MONDAY

19 TUESDAY

20 WEDNESDAY

21 THURSDAY

August
2025

22 FRIDAY

23 SATURDAY

MAKE SOME HOMEMADE, FREEZER-FRIENDLY lunchbox treats to replace packaged options. Try cheese scrolls, oat cookies, muffins, zucchini slice or pikelets.

24 SUNDAY

JULY						
S	M	T	W	T	F	S
		1	2	3	4	5
6	7	8	9	10	11	12
13	14	15	16	17	18	19
20	21	22	23	24	25	26
27	28	29	30	31		

AUGUST						
S	M	T	W	T	F	S
31					1	2
3	4	5	6	7	8	9
10	11	12	13	14	15	16
17	18	19	20	21	22	23
24	25	26	27	28	29	30

SEPTEMBER						
S	M	T	W	T	F	S
	1	2	3	4	5	6
7	8	9	10	11	12	13
14	15	16	17	18	19	20
21	22	23	24	25	26	27
28	29	30				

25 MONDAY

26 TUESDAY

27 WEDNESDAY

28 THURSDAY

August
2025

29 FRIDAY

30 SATURDAY

FOSTER OPEN COMMUNICATION with teenagers by listening to what they say, validating their feelings and timing conversations for when they're not tired or distracted.

31 SUNDAY

"

I was pregnant with my
youngest child when I was
diagnosed with metastatic
breast cancer. To watch him
grow every day, now that he's
almost 10, gives me joy and
hope. My journey has led me
to remain positive in the
unknown, be myself, live
life the best I can, and
to trust in God.

Oripa Nabaro,
diagnosed age 36

let's talk about WELLBEING

Take a proactive approach to your mental health and wellbeing by identifying your stress points, making time for meaningful connection and adopting positive lifestyle choices.

Relationship difficulties, moving house, financial worries, chronic illness or major life changes – these are just some of the things that can make us feel stressed. Stress is a natural response when we feel unable to cope when faced with a challenging situation or event. Everyone's stress levels and triggers are different, and in small doses, stress is nothing to worry about. However, prolonged exposure to stress can affect our sleep, appetite and cardiovascular health, and may lead to more severe mental health conditions like burnout, anxiety and depression. Avoid falling victim to stress with these tips.

Simple strategies to manage stress

ROUTINE Our minds like predictability, familiarity and certainty, so when life gets stressful, establish order with structure and routines that work for you.

PRIORITISE Take a step back from that stressful workload or long to-do list and determine which tasks are most important or most achievable, and tick those off first.

EXERCISE Physical activity stimulates the production of endorphins (feel-good hormones) and restricts cortisol output (adrenalin). Aim for 30 minutes a day.

RELAX Try some relaxation techniques, such as yoga, meditation, deep breathing or listening to music, to help calm your mind and body.

ENJOY During times of stress, find an activity that will help you feel better, be it gardening, reading, sewing or swimming.

CONNECT Spend time with people who make you happy, either face to face or chatting over the phone. It can be incredibly helpful to talk through your worries with someone you trust.

REFLECT Put things in perspective by thinking about what you've accomplished today, the things that made you happy and everything you're grateful for.

AVOID Limit your consumption of caffeine, alcohol and recreational drugs, and avoid social media and news exposure if they trigger stress for you.

For more information, visit Lifeline Australia; lifeline.org.au

A snapshot of women's mental health in Australia

According to the ABS National Study of Mental Health and Wellbeing, 45 per cent of Australian women aged 16 and over have experienced a mental health disorder at some stage in their lives, the most common being depression, anxiety, body image issues, post-traumatic stress disorder, perinatal depression and eating disorders. Certain health issues and life experiences affecting women – from puberty, to pregnancy and childbirth, infertility issues, motherhood and menopause – can take a toll on our mental wellbeing. Factors like poverty, isolation, discrimination, domestic violence and unemployment can also contribute.

KEY STATISTICS SURROUNDING WOMEN'S MENTAL HEALTH

1 IN 3 WOMEN will experience anxiety.

1 IN 6 WOMEN will experience depression or postnatal depression.

WOMEN ARE 2 TIMES MORE LIKELY to experience post-traumatic stress disorder (PTSD) than men.

2 IN 5 WOMEN experience body image issues.

15% OF WOMEN will experience an eating disorder.

21.6% OF WOMEN see a health professional for their mental health.

SO HOW CAN WE CHANGE THIS PICTURE?

Look for the signs. If someone you know is showing persistent signs of sadness or hopelessness, you notice changes in their mood, energy levels or appetite or they become socially withdrawn, reach out and encourage them to find support.

Talk about it. Challenge the stigmas, biases and myths around mental health, particularly for older generations, by sharing your mental health experiences and encouraging friends and loved ones to confide in you if they're having a hard time.

Model positive wellbeing. Set young people up for a positive future by modelling behaviours that help create a healthy mindset, such as making time for self-care, asking for help and supporting others.

Foster connection. A healthy support network is important for wellbeing. Build your 'village' by putting time into existing friendships and building new connections.

IF YOU OR SOMEONE YOU KNOW IS IN CRISIS, please call Lifeline (13 11 14), 13YARN (13 92 76) for Aboriginal and Torres Strait Islander people or Kids Helpline (1800 55 1800) for kids, teens and young adults. Speak to your GP and request a mental health plan to access funding for treatment.

5 myths about depression

Depression rates are on the rise in Australia, but there are a number of misconceptions and misunderstandings that may prevent those affected from seeking treatment. People with depression can feel sad, numb, hopeless or withdrawn for prolonged periods of time. If these feelings don't pass or begin to interfere with your life, it's important to seek help from a health professional. Here, we debunk five common misunderstandings around depression to encourage better understanding for those who need it most.

MYTH #1 **Depression isn't a real illness**
Many people mistake depression for mere sadness, however depression can also affect our physical health. Depression can be triggered by a single event or biological, psychological, social and lifestyle factors.

MYTH #2 **It's best to keep your feelings to yourself** Some people believe that talking about mental illness can "feed the problem". But suffering in silence can be even more harmful. Talking openly about your thoughts and feelings is a crucial part of diagnosis and treatment.

MYTH #3 **Depression is a sign of weakness** Those with depression might struggle to get out of bed, miss school or work or avoid taking part in activities they used to enjoy. From the outside, this might be seen as laziness, and this judgement can add to their feelings of hopelessness, and be detrimental to them seeking help.

MYTH #4 **Antidepressants are the only cure** It's thought antidepressants increase beneficial neurotransmitters in our brain to improve mood and emotion. However, they are usually prescribed in conjunction with long-term strategies, such as therapy, social connection, exercise, eating well and healthy sleep habits. Speak to your doctor to find the best treatment for you.

MYTH #5 **You just need to snap out of it**
There's a common misconception that people can cure their mental illness with a bit of willpower, discipline and positive thinking. However, just like physical medical conditions, depression can't be simply willed away and requires treatment and time.

Easy ways to boost your happiness

The happiness we feel when we spend time with loved ones, achieve our goals or go on holidays comes from our brain releasing one of four chemicals: dopamine, oxytocin, serotonin or endorphins. While we can't feel happy every minute of the day, try these ideas to prompt the production of these hormones and boost your overall enjoyment of life.

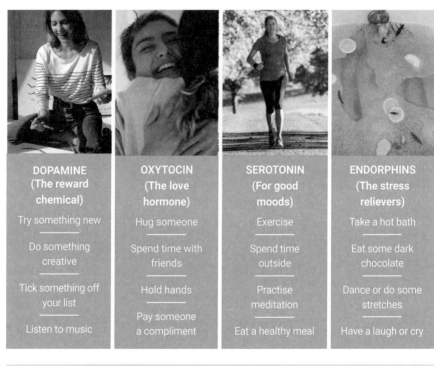

DOPAMINE (The reward chemical)	OXYTOCIN (The love hormone)	SEROTONIN (For good moods)	ENDORPHINS (The stress relievers)
Try something new	Hug someone	Exercise	Take a hot bath
Do something creative	Spend time with friends	Spend time outside	Eat some dark chocolate
Tick something off your list	Hold hands	Practise meditation	Dance or do some stretches
Listen to music	Pay someone a compliment	Eat a healthy meal	Have a laugh or cry

ADHD diagnosis in women

Around 800,000 Australians are currently living with attention deficit hyperactivity disorder (ADHD). Characterised by inattentive, hyperactive and/or impulse behaviours, ADHD is the most common mental health condition in children aged four to 17, and many will continue to experience its effects in adulthood.

ADHD can sometimes be missed in girls and women, who tend to present with more inattentive symptoms (easily distracted, disorganised, forgetful) rather than hyperactive (talking too much, impaired impulse control, fidgeting). These inattentive symptoms are less disruptive and easier to mask (hide from others), and are sometimes mistaken for other conditions, including anxiety and post-traumatic stress disorder. As a result, many women are diagnosed later in life. See your healthcare provider for a potential diagnosis and care plan.

For more information, visit the ADHD Foundation; adhdfoundation.org.au

Wellbeing strategies for later in life

As we get older, health issues, social or physical isolation, personal loss and grief and reduced mobility and independence can all affect our enjoyment of life and increase the risk of anxiety and depression. But with the right supports and solutions, we can enjoy life for many years to come. Here's how.

TAKE CARE OF YOURSELF

Addressing your basic needs of tasty, nutritious meals, regular activity and a good night's sleep can do wonders for your mental state. Seek advice from an exercise professional on which activities are best for you, or sign up for food delivery services if motivation or mobility are an issue.

MAINTAIN CONNECTIONS

Keep feelings of loneliness and isolation at bay by planning catch-ups with friends and family. If face to face isn't possible, try writing letters or emails, chatting on the phone, messaging over WhatsApp or using video options like FaceTime and Zoom.

WIDEN YOUR SOCIAL CIRCLES

If location or circumstances have reduced your friendship group, look for ways to find new connections. Visit your local library or community centre to see what events they have coming up. Trial a few activities and groups to find one you like.

FIND NEW MEANING AND PURPOSE

Keep your mind sharp and fill your days by engaging in tasks like reading, writing, playing music or knitting. Take a class on a subject that interests you, start a new hobby or volunteer to foster a sense of purpose and achievement.

SEEK AND ACCEPT HELP

Asking for help isn't a sign of weakness and doesn't place a burden on others. In fact, it can make life better. Reach out to family and friends, attend support groups or talk to a health professional about your feelings and investigate if you qualify for benefits through My Aged Care.

A U G U S T						
S	M	T	W	T	F	S
31					1	2
3	4	5	6	7	8	9
10	11	12	13	14	15	16
17	18	19	20	21	22	23
24	25	26	27	28	29	30

S E P T E M B E R						
S	M	T	W	T	F	S
	1	2	3	4	5	6
7	8	9	10	11	12	13
14	15	16	17	18	19	20
21	22	23	24	25	26	27
28	29	30				

O C T O B E R						
S	M	T	W	T	F	S
			1	2	3	4
5	6	7	8	9	10	11
12	13	14	15	16	17	18
19	20	21	22	23	24	25
26	27	28	29	30	31	

1 MONDAY

2 TUESDAY

3 WEDNESDAY

4 THURSDAY

September
2025

5 FRIDAY MILAD UN NABI (PROPHET'S BIRTHDAY)

6 SATURDAY

LIVING IN A CLUTTERED SPACE can affect our anxiety levels, sleep and ability to focus. Set aside time each week to sort through one space and get on top of clutter.

7 SUNDAY FATHER'S DAY

AUGUST

S	M	T	W	T	F	S
31					1	2
3	4	5	6	7	8	9
10	11	12	13	14	15	16
17	18	19	20	21	22	23
24	25	26	27	28	29	30

SEPTEMBER

S	M	T	W	T	F	S
	1	2	3	4	5	6
7	8	9	10	11	12	13
14	15	16	17	18	19	20
21	22	23	24	25	26	27
28	29	30				

OCTOBER

S	M	T	W	T	F	S
			1	2	3	4
5	6	7	8	9	10	11
12	13	14	15	16	17	18
19	20	21	22	23	24	25
26	27	28	29	30	31	

8 MONDAY

9 TUESDAY

10 WEDNESDAY

11 THURSDAY R U OK? DAY

September 2025

12 FRIDAY

13 SATURDAY

> **HAVING A SENSE OF DIRECTION,** optimism and hope makes us happier, so book a holiday, buy tickets to a show or set small goals for the week or month ahead.

14 SUNDAY

		A U G U S T							S E P T E M B E R								O C T O B E R				
S	M	T	W	T	F	S	S	M	T	W	T	F	S	S	M	T	W	T	F	S
31					1	2		1	2	3	4	5	6					1	2	3	4
3	4	5	6	7	8	9	7	8	9	10	11	12	13	5	6	7	8	9	10	11
10	11	12	13	14	15	16	14	15	16	17	18	19	20	12	13	14	15	16	17	18
17	18	19	20	21	22	23	21	22	23	24	25	26	27	19	20	21	22	23	24	25
24	25	26	27	28	29	30	28	29	30					26	27	28	29	30	31	

15 MONDAY

16 TUESDAY

17 WEDNESDAY

18 THURSDAY

September
2025

19 FRIDAY

20 SATURDAY

21 SUNDAY

	A U G U S T								S E P T E M B E R								O C T O B E R					
S	M	T	W	T	F	S		S	M	T	W	T	F	S		S	M	T	W	T	F	S
31					1	2			1	2	3	4	5	6					1	2	3	4
3	4	5	6	7	8	9		7	8	9	10	11	12	13		5	6	7	8	9	10	11
10	11	12	13	14	15	16		14	15	16	17	18	19	20		12	13	14	15	16	17	18
17	18	19	20	21	22	23		21	22	23	24	25	26	27		19	20	21	22	23	24	25
24	25	26	27	28	29	30		28	29	30						26	27	28	29	30	31	

22 MONDAY

23 TUESDAY ROSH HASHANAH (JEWISH NEW YEAR)

24 WEDNESDAY

25 THURSDAY

September
2025

26 FRIDAY

27 SATURDAY

FEELING STRESSED? Try sipping a cup of chamomile tea, eating a banana, snacking on nuts or eating two squares of dark chocolate to help regulate mood and lower stress hormones.

28 SUNDAY

WHY I SUPPORT BREAST CANCER TRIALS

With more clinical trials, it's going to get easier to treat and people like me won't have to sit awake at three in the morning, holding their newborn baby, crying and wondering if they will see them grow up. We will know we are safe – and that we can live for our children in more than stories and photographs.

Molly Clayton, diagnosed age 33,
pictured with her children

let's talk about
BREAST HEALTH

One in seven Australian women will be diagnosed with breast cancer at some stage in their lives, but knowing the risk factors, detecting symptoms early and supporting crucial research can all assist in a positive outcome.

Breasts come in all shapes and sizes, and can change at various stages in our lives, from puberty to pregnancy, into menopause and as we get older. Follow these steps to give your breasts the care they need.

4 WAYS TO CARE FOR YOUR BREASTS

1 **Book in for a professional bra fitting.** Up to 80 per cent of women are wearing the wrong bra size, which can lead to back, neck and shoulder pain, chafing, bad posture and breast tissue damage. Weight fluctuations, pregnancy, menopause, changes in exercise routine and age can all cause us to go up or down in bra size, and it's recommended that women be professionally measured for a bra every 12 months.

2 **Get to know your breasts.** Early detection of breast cancer saves lives, and the first step is to become familiar with the look and feel of your breasts through regular self-checks. Not all breast changes will be cancerous, but it's important to be vigilant nonetheless. If you detect any changes, book in to see your GP straightaway. See over the page for the changes to look out for.

3 **Take extra care while breastfeeding.** It's normal to experience a little pain, swelling or tenderness when you first start breastfeeding, and hot and cold compresses, massage and nipple cream may help with this. However, if your breasts become red, hot or painful, or nipples are cracked and bleeding, seek advice from your healthcare professional.

4 **Stay on top of your mammograms.** Our breast cancer risk increases with age, and all women aged 50-74 are eligible for a free two-yearly screening mammogram through BreastScreen Australia. There are over 750 locations across the country and you'll receive a reminder when you're due. Women aged 40-49 and over 75 are also eligible, but won't receive the reminders.

How to manage your breast cancer risk

There are a number of factors that can increase our risk of developing breast cancer, many of which we have no control over. But there are some factors that can be altered to reduce our risk. There are no guarantees, and having a risk factor does not mean you will get breast cancer, and similarly, many women diagnosed with breast cancer have no known risk factors. Your best defence is to read up on the main causes of breast cancer and make positive changes to reduce your risk.

THE RISK FACTORS WE CAN'T CHANGE	
Age	The average age of breast cancer diagnosis in Australia is 61, with around 79 per cent of cases occurring in women aged 50 and older. However, it's important to know that no age group is immune, with many younger women also diagnosed with breast cancer.
Height	Being tall in adulthood comes with a slightly increased risk for breast cancer, with the risk increasing by approximately 17 per cent for every additional 10cm over 175cm.
Breast density	Increased breast density (large amounts of dense glandular tissue) is associated with a higher risk and can only be detected via a mammogram.
Family history	Women with one or more blood relative diagnosed with breast cancer, on their mother's or father's side, have a higher risk, particularly if the relative was diagnosed before the age of 50. The inheritance of breast gene mutations, such as BRCA1, BRCA2, PALB2 and CHEK2, can further increase this risk.
Reproductive factors	Starting your first period before the age of 12, having children after the age of 30 or not having children, and going through late menopause after the age of 55 all bring a slightly higher risk.
Medical history	A previous breast cancer diagnosis, past history of chest radiotherapy for Hodgkin lymphoma or non-cancerous breast conditions and the use of menopausal hormone therapy (MHT) may increase your risk. See your GP.
THE RISK FACTORS WE CAN CHANGE	
Alcohol	The more alcohol you drink, the greater your risk of developing breast cancer. Research indicates there is no safe level when it comes to alcohol consumption, so switch to non-alcoholic alternatives where possible.
Smoking	Smoking has been shown to increase the risk of a number of serious health conditions including breast cancer. To quit, call 137 848.
Weight	Women who are overweight or obese, particularly after menopause, are at an increased risk of breast cancer. You can address this by eating a healthy diet and enjoying regular exercise.
Physical inactivity	Women who don't do any exercise are at a higher risk of breast cancer than those who do. Follow the guidelines of at least 30 minutes of moderate or vigorous activity every day to reverse the risk.

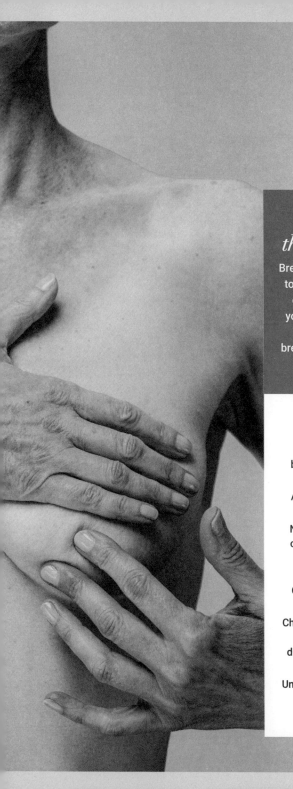

Breast cancer: the signs to look for

Breast awareness is an essential tool in detecting breast cancer early, regardless of how old you are. By being aware of the usual look and feel of your breasts, you can quickly identify any changes that may need further investigation.

SEE YOUR GP IF YOU NOTICE ANY OF THE FOLLOWING:

A new lump or thickening in the breast, armpit or collarbone area

———

A change in breast shape or size

———

Nipple changes, such as sores or crusting, ulcers, inverted nipples, pain, redness or tenderness

———

Clear or bloody nipple discharge

———

Changes to the breast skin including redness, puckering, scaliness, dimpling or other colour variations

———

Unusual tenderness, pain or swelling in the breast or armpit area that doesn't go away.

Dealing with a breast cancer diagnosis

Even with a firm understanding of the risk factors, symptoms and latest research, little can prepare you for the words "you have breast cancer". Every woman's journey with the disease is unique, with age, menopausal status and the type, size and stage of the cancer all determining the best treatment options and strategies. You may experience a range of emotions in the days, weeks and months following your diagnosis, along with uncertainty and anxiety as you navigate the next steps. Try these ideas to make the process a little easier.

TAKE YOUR TIME
It's not easy sharing a cancer diagnosis with family, friends and colleagues, and you should do so in your own time. When you're ready, choose a quiet time and place and be prepared for their questions. Ask for help sharing the news with others beyond your inner circle and only share the information you want to.

FIND A GOOD MEDICAL TEAM
Your specialist can help arrange a team of health professionals (also known as a multidisciplinary team) to drive your treatment based on your needs and preferences. This may include a surgeon, medical oncologist, radiation oncologist, breast care nurse and oncology nurse. Take your time finding the right people, as you will be seeing them on an ongoing basis throughout your treatment and for follow-up appointments.

ACCEPT HELP AND SUPPORT
You don't need to go through this alone, and you'll no doubt have plenty of people offering to help. Let your partner, family and friends assist with everyday tasks like cooking meals, caring for children or doing the housework so you can focus on your treatment. Consider joining a cancer support group or speaking with a psychologist to ease the emotional burden.

TAKE CARE OF YOURSELF
Eating a healthy diet, exercising when you feel up to it and getting enough rest will help your body get through treatment and recovery. Remind yourself that there will be good days and bad days, and make time to do the things you enjoy.

Your support matters

Breast cancer is the most commonly diagnosed cancer for females in Australia, with an estimated 20,500 women affected in 2023. Thankfully, due to an increase in awareness, breast screening and better treatments identified through our research, the rate of survival is also improving. But we still have a way to go before we can eradicate this disease entirely, and your support will play a part in that. All proceeds from the sale of this diary will go towards much-needed clinical trials research to provide a better future for everyone affected by breast cancer.

WHY TRIALS MATTER

Clinical trials research assists in getting the best treatments and tailored approaches to every person diagnosed with and at risk of breast cancer. Clinical trials help to identify new treatment options, prevention strategies and diagnostic tools, as well as ways to address the physical, emotional and financial burden faced by breast cancer patients and their families.

RECENT BREAKTHROUGHS

Breast Cancer Trials has made some exciting discoveries in our recent trials. Notably, our Neo-N clinical trial, which has demonstrated a successful link between the use of immunotherapy, which helps boost the body's own immune system to fight the cancer, in combination with chemotherapy to treat early stage triple negative breast cancer, with 50 per cent of trial participants found to be breast cancer free following treatment. This research outcome is significant as this type of breast cancer currently has the poorest prognosis. The next phase of this trial will aim to build on this new and potentially life-changing knowledge.

WHAT'S NEXT?

Sadly, nine Australian women still lose their lives to breast cancer each day. At Breast Cancer Trials, we are committed to continuing our trials research until no more lives are cut short by breast cancer. Thank you for making this essential work possible.

For more information, visit Breast Cancer Trials; breastcancertrials.org.au

		SEPTEMBER							OCTOBER							NOVEMBER				
S	M	T	W	T	F	S	S	M	T	W	T	F	S	S	M	T	W	T	F	S
	1	2	3	4	5	6				1	2	3	4	30						1
7	8	9	10	11	12	13	5	6	7	8	9	10	11	2	3	4	5	6	7	8
14	15	16	17	18	19	20	12	13	14	15	16	17	18	9	10	11	12	13	14	15
21	22	23	24	25	26	27	19	20	21	22	23	24	25	16	17	18	19	20	21	22
28	29	30					26	27	28	29	30	31		23	24	25	26	27	28	29

29 MONDAY KING'S BIRTHDAY (WA)

30 TUESDAY

1 WEDNESDAY BREAST CANCER AWARENESS MONTH

2 THURSDAY YOM KIPPUR (JEWISH HOLY DAY)

October
2025

3 FRIDAY

4 SATURDAY

5 SUNDAY DAYLIGHT SAVING TIME BEGINS (ACT, NSW, SA, TAS, VIC)

	SEPTEMBER							OCTOBER							NOVEMBER					
S	M	T	W	T	F	S	S	M	T	W	T	F	S	S	M	T	W	T	F	S
	1	2	3	4	5	6				1	2	3	4	30						1
7	8	9	10	11	12	13	5	6	7	8	9	10	11	2	3	4	5	6	7	8
14	15	16	17	18	19	20	12	13	14	15	16	17	18	9	10	11	12	13	14	15
21	22	23	24	25	26	27	19	20	21	22	23	24	25	16	17	18	19	20	21	22
28	29	30					26	27	28	29	30	31		23	24	25	26	27	28	29

6 MONDAY LABOUR DAY (ACT, NSW, SA), KING'S BIRTHDAY (QLD)

7 TUESDAY

8 WEDNESDAY

9 THURSDAY

10 FRIDAY

11 SATURDAY

GET TO KNOW YOUR BREASTS by standing in front of a mirror with your arms by your side and above your head. Take note of any changes during menstruation also.

12 SUNDAY

		SEP	TEM	BER		
S	M	T	W	T	F	S
	1	2	3	4	5	6
7	8	9	10	11	12	13
14	15	16	17	18	19	20
21	22	23	24	25	26	27
28	29	30				

		OC	TO	BER		
S	M	T	W	T	F	S
			1	2	3	4
5	6	7	8	9	10	11
12	13	14	15	16	17	18
19	20	21	22	23	24	25
26	27	28	29	30	31	

		NO	VEM	BER		
S	M	T	W	T	F	S
30						1
2	3	4	5	6	7	8
9	10	11	12	13	14	15
16	17	18	19	20	21	22
23	24	25	26	27	28	29

13 MONDAY

14 TUESDAY

15 WEDNESDAY

16 THURSDAY

October
2025

17 FRIDAY

18 SATURDAY

19 SUNDAY

	SEPTEMBER							OCTOBER							NOVEMBER					
S	M	T	W	T	F	S	S	M	T	W	T	F	S	S	M	T	W	T	F	S
	1	2	3	4	5	6				1	2	3	4	30						1
7	8	9	10	11	12	13	5	6	7	8	9	10	11	2	3	4	5	6	7	8
14	15	16	17	18	19	20	12	13	14	15	16	17	18	9	10	11	12	13	14	15
21	22	23	24	25	26	27	19	20	21	22	23	24	25	16	17	18	19	20	21	22
28	29	30					26	27	28	29	30	31		23	24	25	26	27	28	29

20 MONDAY

21 TUESDAY DIWALI (HINDU, BUDDHIST, JAIN AND SIKH FESTIVAL)

22 WEDNESDAY

23 THURSDAY ROYAL HOBART SHOW (TAS)

October
2025

24 FRIDAY

25 SATURDAY

26 SUNDAY

			SEPTEMBER			
S	M	T	W	T	F	S
		1	2	3	4	5	6
7	8	9	10	11	12	13
14	15	16	17	18	19	20
21	22	23	24	25	26	27
28	29	30				

			OCTOBER			
S	M	T	W	T	F	S
				1	2	3	4
5	6	7	8	9	10	11
12	13	14	15	16	17	18
19	20	21	22	23	24	25
26	27	28	29	30	31	

			NOVEMBER			
S	M	T	W	T	F	S
30						1
2	3	4	5	6	7	8
9	10	11	12	13	14	15
16	17	18	19	20	21	22
23	24	25	26	27	28	29

27 MONDAY AUSTRALIA'S BREAST CANCER DAY

28 TUESDAY

29 WEDNESDAY

30 THURSDAY

October–November
2025

31 FRIDAY <small>HALLOWEEN</small>

SWITCH TO A SPORTS BRA
when exercising to prevent breast pain, reduce movement and protect the delicate tissue and ligaments. Book in for a fitting to find the right type.

1 SATURDAY

2 SUNDAY

" Breast cancer has struck my family over three generations. My grandmothe[r] died aged 52 leaving my mother and her siblings to cope with life without her. Then my aunty also died from breast cancer aged 42, leaving three young children. And now me. We need more research to stop it here, so tha[t] I can live a long, happy life and to protect my children's generation.

Naomi Richards, diagnosed age 40

let's talk about
HEALTHY SKIN

Sun exposure, stress, diet and hormonal changes can all take a toll on our skin. Practise sun safety and establish some good skincare habits to put your best face forward in more ways than one.

When unprotected skin is exposed to UV radiation, it can damage the skin cells and change the way they look and behave. In some cases, this can lead to skin cancer. You can't always see or feel this damage and it can add up over time. UV radiation can be high even on cool or overcast days.

THE TYPES There are three main types of skin cancer: basal cell carcinoma (BCC) and squamous cell carcinoma (SCC), which are classed as non-melanoma skin cancers and make up 99 per cent of skin cancers; and melanoma, which is the more serious form because it can quickly spread to other parts of the body if not found or treated early.

WHO IS AT RISK? Anyone can develop skin cancer, although those with pale or freckled skin, red or fair hair and blue or green eyes have an increased risk. People who work outdoors, sunbake, use solariums or are repeatedly exposed to UV radiation are more likely to develop skin cancer. Having a weakened immune system, a previous or family history of skin cancer and smoking can also make you more susceptible. If you have brown, black, olive or very dark skin, you can still develop skin cancer.

THE STATS
- At least two in three Australians will be diagnosed with some form of skin cancer before the age of 70.
- Australia has one of the highest rates of skin cancer in the world.
- Over 95% of skin cancers are caused by UV radiation exposure.
- Over one million treatments are given each year for non-melanoma skin cancers.
- Non-melanoma skin cancers can affect young people, but are more common in those aged 40 and over.
- Around 2000 Australians die from skin cancer each year.

YOUR PROTECTION PLAN
- Check the UV Index in your area using the Cancer Council's free SunSmart app whenever you're heading outside.
- Use sun-safe measures (see 'How to be sun safe' over the page) to protect your skin when UV levels are 3 or higher.
- Regularly monitor for any changes to existing freckles, moles and spots as well as new spots. If you notice any variation in colour, size, texture or shape, or if spots become tender, sore or itchy, see your GP or a dermatologist to have it checked. You'll have a better outcome if a skin cancer is found and treated early.

For more information, visit The Australasian College of Dermatologists; dermcoll.edu.au

How to be sun safe

Take these steps to protect your skin from the sun's damaging UV rays

Slip on sun-protective clothing

When out in the sun, wear items of clothing that cover as much skin as possible, such as long-sleeved collared shirts, loose pants, long skirts or rash vests. Darker fabrics and those with an ultraviolet protection factor (UPF) of 50 or above are ideal.

Slop on some sunscreen

Apply an SPF 30+ (or higher) broad-spectrum, water-resistant sunscreen 20 minutes before going outdoors and every two hours after, or sooner if you've been swimming, sweating or the sunscreen has rubbed off. Adults need seven teaspoons for a full body application – one teaspoon per arm and leg (four in total), one each for the front and back of the body and another teaspoon to cover the face, neck and ears.

Slap on a hat

Look for a legionnaire, broad-brimmed or bucket style hat to shade your head, face, neck, eyes and ears. Avoid loose-weave fabrics, baseball caps and sun visors as they don't offer full protection.

Slide on some sunglasses

Protect your eyes and the delicate skin around them with a pair of close-fitting, wraparound sunglasses that meet Australian Standards. These should be worn all year round.

Seek shade

Shelter under the shade of trees, umbrellas, buildings or canopies. UV radiation can reflect off surfaces like concrete, water, sand and snow, so this should be done in combination with the other four steps.

Simple changes for healthy skin

The skin plays an important role in protecting our bodies from germs and disease, so we want to keep it as healthy as possible. Harsh chemicals, diet, hormones, the weather and damaging UV rays can play havoc with our complexions – counteract them with some simple tricks.

STAY HYDRATED Drinking plenty of fluids (the recommendation is two litres of water a day) can help flush the body of toxins for a healthy glow. Track your intake using a water bottle with measurements down the side and add berries, sliced lemon or fresh herbs to improve the taste.

WASH YOUR FACE It goes without saying, but sometimes when we're tired or in a rush, we can skip this step. Make face-washing a habit in the morning to remove bacteria and dirt accumulated overnight and at the end of the day to remove make-up and grime. Wash after sweating, too.

WEAR GLOVES Keep the skin on your hands soft and callous-free by wearing gloves when you wash the dishes, clean the bathroom and work in the garden, and when you're spending time outside on cold days.

TAKE COOL SHOWERS Hot water can be incredibly drying for skin, so the cooler your shower temperature, the better. Cold water also increases blood flow to the skin. After you've finished in the shower, blot your skin dry (don't rub) and finish off with a body lotion to seal in moisture.

TAN SAFELY If you like the bronzed look, book in for a spray tan or use a self-tanning lotion rather than sunbaking or using solariums. Remember, tanning products won't protect your skin from UV radiation, so apply a SPF 50+ sunscreen on top before heading outside.

DON'T SMOKE Smoking and vaping speeds up the ageing process and damages the skin's collagen and elastin layers. It can also exacerbate skin conditions like acne, psoriasis and pigmentation.

GET YOUR BEAUTY SLEEP The skin repairs itself at night, so the more sleep you get, the more time it has to replenish. Getting a restful eight hours of sleep a night can also reduce under-eye shadows and puffiness.

EXFOLIATE Skin cell renewal slows down as we age, clogging pores and leading to a dull complexion. To remove dead cells, apply exfoliator using a gentle, circular motion (rigorous scrubbing can irritate the skin) two to three times a week.

How the environment affects our skin

As our body's largest organ, the skin provides a layer of protection against harmful nanoparticles, bacteria and chemicals. But it's not invincible, and prolonged and repeated exposure to environmental factors like weather conditions, smoking and pollution can make the skin prone to inflammation, which can cause uneven skin tone, pigmentation, acne and advanced wrinkles. Indeed, research has found that people living in cities suffer from wrinkles and age spots earlier than their rural counterparts due to higher levels of pollution, with mature skin particularly sensitive to these environmental stressors.

Pollution takes many forms, from car exhaust fumes, smoke and fine dust particles in the air, to chemicals in the water. And it's impossible to know what damage these invisible particles are doing until it's too late. But there are steps you can take to protect your skin now.

3 STEPS TO PROTECT SKIN FROM ENVIRONMENTAL AGGRESSORS

1 **WASH YOUR FACE EVERY DAY.** This will remove any grime or pollution that can sit on the skin's surface and penetrate the pores.

2 **LATHER ON A BARRIER CREAM.** The easiest way to do this is with an SPF 50+ sunscreen, which will protect you from pollution and the sun's harmful UV rays. Look for one that boasts environmental protection or an anti-pollution formula on the label.

3 **LOOK TO ANTIOXIDANTS.** Pollution can cause free radicals to develop on the skin, which can damage skin cells, proteins and DNA. Fight them with antioxidants, either in food form like blueberries and leafy greens, or as an ingredient in face oils and serums.

Delivering the Goods

By sending books to First Nations children, supporting mental wellbeing and raising funds in times of disaster, we're supporting communities in every corner of the country.

auspost.com.au

		OCTOBER							NOVEMBER							DECEMBER			
S	M	T	W	T	F	S	S	M	T	W	T	F	S	S	M	T	W	T	F	S
			1	2	3	4	30						1		1	2	3	4	5	6
5	6	7	8	9	10	11	2	3	4	5	6	7	8	7	8	9	10	11	12	13
12	13	14	15	16	17	18	9	10	11	12	13	14	15	14	15	16	17	18	19	20
19	20	21	22	23	24	25	16	17	18	19	20	21	22	21	22	23	24	25	26	27
26	27	28	29	30	31		23	24	25	26	27	28	29	28	29	30	31			

3 MONDAY RECREATION DAY (TAS)

4 TUESDAY MELBOURNE CUP DAY (VIC)

5 WEDNESDAY

6 THURSDAY

7 FRIDAY

8 SATURDAY

MAKE A TIME TO REGULARLY CHECK YOUR MOLES and spots for changes. Set a calendar reminder for the first day of each month or make a habit of checking at the beginning of each season.

9 SUNDAY

		OCTOBER							NOVEMBER							DECEMBER				
S	M	T	W	T	F	S	S	M	T	W	T	F	S	S	M	T	W	T	F	S
			1	2	3	4	30						1		1	2	3	4	5	6
5	6	7	8	9	10	11	2	3	4	5	6	7	8	7	8	9	10	11	12	13
12	13	14	15	16	17	18	9	10	11	12	13	14	15	14	15	16	17	18	19	20
19	20	21	22	23	24	25	16	17	18	19	20	21	22	21	22	23	24	25	26	27
26	27	28	29	30	31		23	24	25	26	27	28	29	28	29	30	31			

10 MONDAY

11 TUESDAY REMEMBRANCE DAY

12 WEDNESDAY

13 THURSDAY

November
2025

14 FRIDAY

15 SATURDAY

LEAVE A LASTING LEGACY by leaving a gift in your will. Visit breastcancetrials. org.au or call 1800 423 444 for more information.

16 SUNDAY

OCTOBER
S	M	T	W	T	F	S
			1	2	3	4
5	6	7	8	9	10	11
12	13	14	15	16	17	18
19	20	21	22	23	24	25
26	27	28	29	30	31	

NOVEMBER
S	M	T	W	T	F	S
30						1
2	3	4	5	6	7	8
9	10	11	12	13	14	15
16	17	18	19	20	21	22
23	24	25	26	27	28	29

DECEMBER
S	M	T	W	T	F	S
	1	2	3	4	5	6
7	8	9	10	11	12	13
14	15	16	17	18	19	20
21	22	23	24	25	26	27
28	29	30	31			

17 MONDAY

18 TUESDAY

19 WEDNESDAY

20 THURSDAY

21 FRIDAY

22 SATURDAY

DON'T KEEP SUNSCREEN IN THE CAR. The active ingredients break down when exposed to heat. Instead, keep a tube in your handbag, desk drawer or by the front door.

23 SUNDAY

		OCTOBER							NOVEMBER							DECEMBER				
S	M	T	W	T	F	S	S	M	T	W	T	F	S	S	M	T	W	T	F	S
			1	2	3	4	30						1		1	2	3	4	5	6
5	6	7	8	9	10	11	2	3	4	5	6	7	8	7	8	9	10	11	12	13
12	13	14	15	16	17	18	9	10	11	12	13	14	15	14	15	16	17	18	19	20
19	20	21	22	23	24	25	16	17	18	19	20	21	22	21	22	23	24	25	26	27
26	27	28	29	30	31		23	24	25	26	27	28	29	28	29	30	31			

24 MONDAY

25 TUESDAY

26 WEDNESDAY

27 THURSDAY

November
2025

28 FRIDAY

29 SATURDAY

STRESS SHOWS ON OUR SKIN. Help mitigate it by getting a good night's sleep, setting reasonable limits on your time and making room for things you enjoy.

30 SUNDAY

66

My treatment can be challenging and leave me feeling weak and anxious at times. I'm thankful for my partner, children, parents, sisters and extended family who support me and fuel me with the will to recover.

Michelle Mozo,
diagnosed age 47

let's talk about
LIFESTYLE

Our best intentions can disappear towards the end of the year. So why not take this time to reestablish some positive habits or read up on new ways to make your health and wellbeing top priority.

As temperatures soar over summer, it's important to stay hydrated. This is especially important as we get older and our body's ability to recognise thirst and conserve water slowly declines. To stay consistently hydrated, it's recommended that we consume about eight cups (two litres) of water or other fluids throughout each day, however, many people find it difficult to meet this target. Try these tips to stay hydrated and well.

SUMMER HYDRATION TIPS

Make water easily accessible by keeping a glass of water beside your bed, having a jug filled in the fridge and carrying a water bottle with you when you go out.

Eat your fluids. Many fruits and vegetables have a high water content, including cucumber, watermelon, grapes, lettuce, tomatoes and oranges. Steaming vegetables like broccoli, cauliflower and squash also increases their water content.

Watch your urine. This is your body's natural indicator of your hydration levels. A pale, straw-like colour is ideal, while dark yellow or brown urine means you need to increase your fluid intake.

Mix it up. If plain water doesn't appeal, try infusing it with fruit or herbs to improve its taste. Sparkling water, milk, juice, tea and coffee (in moderation) also count towards your daily fluid intake, and in summer, ice blocks and smoothies can be a great alternative (just watch the sugar content).

Make it a challenge. Set hourly reminders on your phone to drink some water or break it up into manageable increments. For example, a glass of water when you wake up, a cup of tea with breakfast, another glass of water before your shower and so on.

Consider your environment. Sitting inside a hot, stuffy house can increase the risk of dehydration, so close blinds and use fans or air-conditioning to cool and ventilate your home. When outside, wear a hat and loose, breathable clothing to keep your body temperature in check.

Easy make-ahead meal ideas

At this busy point of the year – or at any time when you're tired, stressed or unwell – add these healthy meal ideas to your arsenal. All can be pre-prepared and portioned out for the week ahead or frozen for those days when time or energy are lacking.

BREAKFAST

Home-made granola Combine oats, chopped nuts, coconut flakes and chia seeds, drizzle with honey and oven bake until golden. Serve ½ cup of granola with fruit and yoghurt.	**Bacon and egg cups** Mix together eggs, milk, diced tomato, diced bacon and herbs. Bake in a greased muffin pan for 25 minutes. Freeze and reheat; 2 per serve.	**Pancakes** Whisk 1½ cups milk, 2 eggs, 2 cups wholemeal flour and 2 teaspoons sugar. Cook in batches; freeze pancakes between sheets of baking paper. Microwave to reheat.

LUNCH

DIY salads Start with a base of salad leaves, then add legumes, vegetables, rice or pasta (fibre); avocado, nuts or cheese (good fats); and cooked chicken, tuna or boiled egg (protein).	**Chicken & corn soup** Poach chicken in salt-reduced stock. Shred chicken and return to the pot with canned corn; whisk in a beaten egg. Add a dash of low-sodium soy sauce.	**Meatballs** Combine beef, turkey or lamb mince with grated carrot, chopped onion, an egg and breadcrumbs. Shape into meatballs and bake. Serve with salad or roast veg.

DINNER

  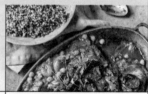

Chilli con carne Saute diced capsicum, onion, garlic and chilli. Brown turkey mince; add diced tomatoes, kidney beans and spices and simmer. Serve with rice, avocado or bread.	**Vegetarian lasagne** Make a ragu from garlic, onion, tomatoes and spinach, layer with lasagne sheets and ricotta and top with mozzarella. Bake until golden.	**Slow-cooker casserole** Make a hearty chicken or beef stew using whatever vegetables you have on hand, diced tomatoes and fresh herbs. Serve with couscous or mash.

5 reasons we need to get more sleep

Getting the right amount of sleep each day is one of the most important things you can do for your health. Sleep gives our bodies a chance to rest, recover and repair. Without enough sleep, our concentration, memory, mood and ability to perform tasks can suffer. Long-term sleep deprivation or disruption, as well as oversleeping, can contribute to a number of serious health problems. Here are five benefits that come from a good night's sleep.

1 Sleep assists in the brain's ability to learn, think clearly, concentrate, pay attention to tasks and make decisions. Sleep deprivation may also increase the risk of Alzheimer's disease and dementia.

2 When the body is at rest, your heart rate slows down and tissue repair and regeneration takes place, reducing strain on the cardiovascular system and revitalising the body and mind.

3 Adequate sleep helps the body's immune system fight against infections and illnesses.

4 Improving sleep may help reduce the risk of mental health concerns like depression and anxiety, which are typically linked with chronic sleep disturbance.

5 Sleep is essential for regulating the hormones that affect hunger and appetite. Limited sleep, on the other hand, can slow down metabolism and increase sugar cravings, resulting in weight gain.

HOW MUCH SLEEP DO WE NEED? Sleep needs vary from person to person, but experts recommend seven to nine hours a night for adults, or seven to eight hours from the age of 65. Children need more, ranging from 14 to 17 hours for newborns, 11 to 14 hours for toddlers, nine to 11 hours for school-aged children and eight to 10 hours for teenagers.

For more information, visit the Sleep Health Foundation; sleephealthfoundation.org.au

Complementary therapies explained

Complementary or alternative therapies are a range of practices not considered part of evidence-based, conventional medicine. They are used to help manage health conditions, counteract symptoms or improve quality of life. Complementary therapies may not provide any benefit and could bring unwanted side effects. Always seek medical advice to minimise the risk of harm.

COMPLEMENTARY VS ALTERNATIVE

Complementary therapies are used alongside conventional medicine, and there is some evidence to suggest they can be beneficial when used this way. Alternative therapies, on the other hand, are used instead of traditional medicine and are typically unproven or have been shown to be ineffective.

SAFETY TIPS

- Consult with your doctor before using a complementary therapy to discuss the risks and decide if it's of benefit to you.
- Always check that your chosen complementary health practitioner is listed with the Australian Health Practitioner Regulation Agency.
- Disclose all medications, therapies and treatments that you're currently using with your health practitioner.
- Never stop taking prescribed medications or change the dose without first discussing with your doctor.
- Be wary of purchasing complementary treatments over the internet. Always buy from a reputable supplier, such as a health food store or pharmacy.

EXAMPLES OF EVIDENCE-BASED COMPLEMENTARY THERAPIES

Acupuncture – for pain relief	A form of traditional Chinese medicine, thin needles are inserted into the skin at specific points to treat a range of disorders.
Aromatherapy – for physical and psychological wellbeing	The use of plant oils, including essential oils, to elicit a physiological or emotional response.
Chiropractic – for pain relief and movement	Chiropractors use their hands to examine and treat problems relating to the bones, muscles and joints.
Herbal medicine – for general health and wellbeing	The use of plants to treat disease and return the body to a natural sense of balance to assist healing.
Hypnosis – for addiction, phobias or anxiety	A method of inducing a state of deep relaxation in order to treat psychological or emotional disorders or addictions.
Massage – for muscular pain and relaxation	The practice of kneading or manipulating the body's soft tissue and muscles to improve wellbeing or health.
Meditation – for mental clarity and wellbeing	A deliberate focusing of attention to bring feelings of calm, energy and awareness.
Naturopathy – for general health and wellbeing	A holistic approach to wellness based around the importance of nutrition, water, sunlight, exercise and stress management.
Osteopathy – for movement and pain relief	A holistic approach to healing, taking the whole musculoskeletal system into account.
Yoga – for physical and mental wellbeing	Utilises gentle movement, meditation and breathing to help relieve stress, manage anxiety and ease pain.

EXCLUSIVE SUBSCRIPTIONS OFFER

THE AUSTRALIAN
Women's Weekly

Subscribe to Australia's most iconic magazine with this exclusive offer!

SIX ISSUES FOR
$47
Save 10%

PERFECT GIFT IDEA

Subscribe & receive

- Six issues of *The Australian Women's Weekly* for $47* once off payment
- **SAVE 10% off** the retail price
- **FREE DELIVERY** to your home each month

2 EASY WAYS TO ORDER

MAGSHOP.COM.AU/AWMHEALTH25   CALL 136 116 and quote M24AWMH

NOVEMBER						
S	M	T	W	T	F	S
30						1
2	3	4	5	6	7	8
9	10	11	12	13	14	15
16	17	18	19	20	21	22
23	24	25	26	27	28	29

DECEMBER						
S	M	T	W	T	F	S
	1	2	3	4	5	6
7	8	9	10	11	12	13
14	15	16	17	18	19	20
21	22	23	24	25	26	27
28	29	30	31			

JANUARY						
S	M	T	W	T	F	S
				1	2	3
4	5	6	7	8	9	10
11	12	13	14	15	16	17
18	19	20	21	22	23	24
25	26	27	28	29	30	31

1 MONDAY

2 TUESDAY

3 WEDNESDAY

4 THURSDAY

December
2025

5 FRIDAY

6 SATURDAY

7 SUNDAY

NOVEMBER
S	M	T	W	T	F	S
30						1
2	3	4	5	6	7	8
9	10	11	12	13	14	15
16	17	18	19	20	21	22
23	24	25	26	27	28	29

DECEMBER
S	M	T	W	T	F	S
	1	2	3	4	5	6
7	8	9	10	11	12	13
14	15	16	17	18	19	20
21	22	23	24	25	26	27
28	29	30	31			

JANUARY
S	M	T	W	T	F	S
				1	2	3
4	5	6	7	8	9	10
11	12	13	14	15	16	17
18	19	20	21	22	23	24
25	26	27	28	29	30	31

8 MONDAY

9 TUESDAY

10 WEDNESDAY

11 THURSDAY

December
2025

12 FRIDAY

13 SATURDAY

FOR OPTIMAL HYDRATION, have small sips of water throughout the day rather than gulping down one glass at a time. Room temperature water is best for digestion.

14 SUNDAY

NOVEMBER						
S	M	T	W	T	F	S
30						1
2	3	4	5	6	7	8
9	10	11	12	13	14	15
16	17	18	19	20	21	22
23	24	25	26	27	28	29

DECEMBER						
S	M	T	W	T	F	S
	1	2	3	4	5	6
7	8	9	10	11	12	13
14	15	16	17	18	19	20
21	22	23	24	25	26	27
28	29	30	31			

JANUARY						
S	M	T	W	T	F	S
				1	2	3
4	5	6	7	8	9	10
11	12	13	14	15	16	17
18	19	20	21	22	23	24
25	26	27	28	29	30	31

15 MONDAY HANUKKAH BEGINS

16 TUESDAY

17 WEDNESDAY

18 THURSDAY

December
2025

19 FRIDAY

20 SATURDAY

ENJOYING A NAP DURING THE DAY counts towards your seven to nine hours of sleep and has been found to alleviate cognitive deficits, but limit it to no longer than 30 minutes.

21 SUNDAY

NOVEMBER						
S	M	T	W	T	F	S
30						1
2	3	4	5	6	7	8
9	10	11	12	13	14	15
16	17	18	19	20	21	22
23	24	25	26	27	28	29

DECEMBER						
S	M	T	W	T	F	S
	1	2	3	4	5	6
7	8	9	10	11	12	13
14	15	16	17	18	19	20
21	22	23	24	25	26	27
28	29	30	31			

JANUARY						
S	M	T	W	T	F	S
				1	2	3
4	5	6	7	8	9	10
11	12	13	14	15	16	17
18	19	20	21	22	23	24
25	26	27	28	29	30	31

22 MONDAY

23 TUESDAY

24 WEDNESDAY CHRISTMAS EVE

25 THURSDAY CHRISTMAS DAY

December
2025

26 FRIDAY BOXING DAY, PROCLAMATION DAY (SA)

27 SATURDAY

WITH THE YEAR DRAWING TO A CLOSE, take the time to reflect on the highs and lows of 2025 and feel gratitude for everything you've experienced.

28 SUNDAY

		NOVEMBER				
S	M	T	W	T	F	S
30						1
2	3	4	5	6	7	8
9	10	11	12	13	14	15
16	17	18	19	20	21	22
23	24	25	26	27	28	29

		DECEMBER				
S	M	T	W	T	F	S
	1	2	3	4	5	6
7	8	9	10	11	12	13
14	15	16	17	18	19	20
21	22	23	24	25	26	27
28	29	30	31			

		JANUARY				
S	M	T	W	T	F	S
				1	2	3
4	5	6	7	8	9	10
11	12	13	14	15	16	17
18	19	20	21	22	23	24
25	26	27	28	29	30	31

29 MONDAY

30 TUESDAY

31 WEDNESDAY NEW YEAR'S EVE

1 THURSDAY NEW YEAR'S DAY

January
2026

2 FRIDAY

3 SATURDAY

SET SOME ENJOYABLE CHALLENGES for the year ahead, such as trying a new recipe each week, taking a photo of something beautiful every day or visiting a new beach each month.

4 SUNDAY

Notes

Notes

Notes

THE AUSTRALIAN WOMEN'S

Health Diary ®

Editor: Tiffany Dunk

Art & Picture Director: Ellen Erickson

Writer & Copy Editor: Stephanie Hope

BCT Diary Manager: Julie Callaghan

BCT Diary Marketing: Belinda Carrall

Breast Cancer Trials (BCT)

1800 423 444; breastcancertrials.org.au

diaryenquiries@bctrials.org.au

The Australian Women's Health Diary®
is produced by the publishers of
The Australian Women's Weekly on
behalf of Breast Cancer Trials.

Women's Weekly

THE AUSTRALIAN

Editor: Sophie Tedmanson

Chief Executive Officer: Jane Huxley

BREAST CANCER TRIALS

NO MORE LIVES CUT SHORT